Data-Driven Business Models for the Digital Economy

Data-Driven Business Models for the Digital Economy

How Great Companies Run on Data

Rado Kotorov, PhD

Abstract

Today's most valuable digital companies have no physical assets. Data-driven business models scale not through asset accumulation and product standardization, but through disaggregation of supply and demand to cater to the individual preferences of each consumer. The winners in the new economy master the demand for one and the supply to millions. Analytical craftsmanship at scale is replacing the traditional mass production and changing how markets and competition work.

Keywords

digitizatal businesses; business models; data driven companies; data analytics; digital economy; competitive advantage

Contents

Foreword...ix

Part I   **How Digital Giants Are Creating
the New Economy**...1

Chapter 1   The Brave New Digital World 3

Chapter 2   Why Companies Miss Out on Big Opportunities 7

Chapter 3   Everything Is Changing..17

Chapter 4   Scale and Scope in the Digital Economy 27

Chapter 5   The New Economics of Disaggregation and Scale 35

Chapter 6   The Two Market Competition Rules
for the Digital Economy 45

Part II   **Data-Driven Business Models**...................................55

Chapter 7   Asset-Less Business Models 57

Chapter 8   Data Products as a Business...67

Chapter 9   Digital Supplements..79

Chapter 10   The Man-Less Business Model 91

Part III   **The Analytics of Growth**...105

Chapter 11   The Pursuit of Analytics Maturity 107

Chapter 12   Beating the Averages With Trends AI 121

About the Author...133

Index 135

Foreword

Those who spout on about data being the "new oil" are only at the cusp of realizing data's potential, and I find typically are on the outside looking in at those thriving as part of the Information Age and digital economy. When I first met Rado Kotorov a decade ago he was clearly not one of these individuals. We got to talking about the variety of unique economic attributes of information and how it was incumbent upon business leaders to capitalize on them.

Yet even celebrated business leaders sometimes at first fail to understand information's value proposition. In 1996 at the outset of the Internet's Cambrian explosion Steve Jobs remarked, "I don't see most people using the Web to get more information. We're already in information overload." This attitude of information as an annoyance, or at best a nice-to-have resource, has been the death of thousands of companies. The contrarian view of information as a true economic asset, however, has birthed new businesses, business models, digital products and services, and overall marketplaces.

Today these businesses and business models are all around us, at home, at play, at work, and everywhere in between. Taking advantage of them as a consumer is as easy as opening a browser or picking up a smartphone and downloading an app. But taking advantage of them as a business model has proven challenging for many business leaders. Indeed, status quo business processes, methods, and even legacy technologies can inhibit a business from expediently becoming data driven or offering digital solutions. But as Dr. Kotorov points out, it's more about an inability to recognize information as an actual economic asset, to appreciate its unique economic properties, and to change one's mindset. Easier said than done.

Thankfully "Data-Driven Business Models for the Digital Economy" weaves inspirational stories and a roadmap to innovating with information. The first key lesson is to recognize that you don't need physical assets to create equity. My own research into the economics of information (or "infonomics") revealed how investors favor data-savvy businesses with a market-to-book valuations nearly three times higher than traditional businesses. His book goes further to describe how to cannibalize traditional business models, how to "scale and scope" with data, how to introduce data as a product/service, and how to develop digital supplements, and the importance of self-service enablement today.

The earliest known mention of "business intelligence" in Richard Devens and Sinclair Hamilton's 1865 book, "The Cyclopaedia of Commercial and Business Anecdotes," recounts how information about military battles was collected and sold to King William. Today, just as then, information moves markets. But today information has created new markets, new products, new services, and new business models. Data monetization isn't just about selling data, it's about using data to generate all manner of economic benefits. Doubtless new types of benefits already are being conceived by tomorrow's datapreneurs. And for those who have been wondering how to join them, this book is just the guide they have been craving.

Dr. Kotorov's wealth of experience and fresh thinking come through loud and clear and may be just the smack upside the head or kick in the seat of the pants that many business leaders need to lead their organizations to become truly data driven.

Douglas Laney,
Author of *Infonomics: How to Monetize,*
Manage, and Measure Information as an Asset for
Competitive Advantage, Principal Data Strategist, Caserta
Adjunct Professor, University of Illinois Gies School of Business
Three-time Gartner annual Thought Leadership Award recipient

PART I

How Digital Giants Are Creating the New Economy

At Least 40% of all Businesses will die in the next ten years ... If They don't figure out how to change their entire company to accommodate new technologies.
—John Chambers, Executive Chairman, CISCO System

The last ten years of it have been about changing the way people work. The next ten years of it will be about transforming your business.
—Aaron Levie, CEO Of Box

CHAPTER 1

The Brave New Digital World

What do the most popular and most valuable companies today have in common?

These are the companies that are household names, that permeate the news, that have become part of our daily routines and habits, and even part of our language, as some companies' names have become verbs.

These companies:

1. They have millions and even billions of users globally;
2. They own their respective markets, that is, they completely dominate these markets;
3. They are all young companies, founded in the last 20 years;
4. They have enormous market valuations and capitalizations;
5. They continue to grow at double digit rates as they expand and disrupt adjacent markets;
6. Everyone wants to work for one of these companies;
7. Finally, and most importantly, these companies do not own physical assets or if they do, this is not what drives their phenomenal success.

Some people call these companies digital giants[1] because they are built and run on data. They are completely different from the rest of the companies in the economy precisely because they do not have and do not build their business models and their competitive advantages on physical assets. In fact, they view assets as a liability because physical assets take

---

[1] I am not sure who coined the term digital giants. IMD Business School for Management and Leadership Courses started publishing about the top digital giants in 2017, https://imd.org

time and energy to be managed. Physical assets consume expensive management resources which can manage only a limited number of assets. Physical assets are viewed as a distraction from the core business. They are like an old car that is not only costly to fix but also needs fixing quite frequently.

This is not an entirely new way of thinking. When Warren Buffet was starting a family in 1955, he refused to buy a house contrary to "common sense." He was an investor and his reasoning was quite simple and logical:

> In Omaha, I rented a house at 5202 Underwood for $175 a month. I told my wife, "I'd be glad to buy a house, but that's like a carpenter selling his toolkit." I didn't want to use up my capital.[2]

While for many people a house is viewed as an investment, for Buffet it was a liability.

Like Buffet, the digital giants avoid conventional wisdom and do not focus on physical assets—you do not have to buy physical assets to create equity! Instead, the digital giants focus on business models that bypass all together the accumulation of assets, which traditional companies consider to be the biggest barrier to entry for new competitors in their controlled markets. The digital giants are focused on DATA and its magical ability to create value out of itself.

Each one of the digital giants has invented its own data-driven business model. Each one has figured out how to collect or use other people's data and package or repackage these data as useful information that can be sold. But the model to monetize these data is not always so easy to invent.

This is why it is hard for traditional companies to transition to the digital economy. This may just be a coincidence and habit as we are used to creating business models that are tied to physical goods.

The need for search became instantly obvious once the first web pages were launched. You sit in front of a computer screen, you are reading a

---

[2] Randall Lane. 2014. "Warren Buffett's $50 Billion Decision." https://forbes.com/sites/randalllane/2012/03/26/warren-buffetts-50-billion-decision/#7de39bc740cb

page, questions arise, you know there are thousands of pages on the web and many of them may contain relevant information to your questions. How do you get to these pages? It is not difficult to guess that you need a search function. And yet the need to search cannot be monetized directly.

The consumer sees search as a utility, as something that just has to be there to make this entire Web-thing useful. Without it, the World Wide Web is just a walled garden restricted to what you learn from hearsay and what your memory can retain.

And there is a second issue. How do you charge the consumer for searching the web? Charge them for every search or a flat monthly fee? Consumers hate variable costs, that is, those that vary based on usage or how many searches you perform. Consumers like to have more predictable expenditures that they can budget. This is why even gas and electrical utilities switched to plans that stabilize the monthly payments. Consumers did not like the difference between winter and summer monthly utility bills as it disrupted their budgets and hence the utilities had to invent new regular monthly plans. On the other hand, charging a monthly fee for search leaves too much money on the table, as peaks of usage on word searches are hard and expensive to predict. Hence, no consumer wants to pay for search and no pricing model is easy when demand is disaggregated based on the use of words.

These are the big differences from the physical world in which a need can be monetized directly. The need to sleep has created and continues to create different companies that produce beds, pillows, night lamps, blankets and duvets, sleeping accessories, and electronic gadgets. These products directly satisfy needs and consumers pay directly for the products.

Data-driven companies almost never monetize needs directly because of the disintermediation of the demand or the ownership of the resources. Google sells the words from dictionary to advertisers. Facebook sells information about relevant posts to advertisers. Pinterest sells relevant information about our interests and hobbies to advertisers. I do not mean that Facebook and Pinterest sell the actual content which would violate the user's privacy. They sell demographic and psychographic information associated with posts and users that allows advertisers to target particular audiences more accurately. Airbnb, Lyft, and Uber sell a service directly to consumers through an indirect use of resources, because they do not own the cars that provide the service or the properties that they rent. In the data-driven economy the need, the payer, and the ownership of the resources are frequently disintermediated.

Data-driven business models typically leverage information to align multiple different needs to achieve a monetizable business model. Lyft and Uber satisfy two consumer needs—(1) the basic need to find a ride and (2) the basic need of some people to earn extra income. And so do Google, Facebook, and Pinterest, who align basic human needs to find information and share experiences or hobbies with friends, with the need of advertisers to reach targeted audiences.

Throughout this book we will explore how the invention of data-driven business models propels the fortunes of companies in today's digital economy. There is a tremendous variation of data-driven business models that creates invaluable opportunities both for established companies and start-ups. There are asset-less business models, man-less business models, product-less business models, service-less, digital products business models, and many more. Some models are profoundly changing traditional notions of capitalism. Data and analytics are helping companies move from mass production into extreme personalization and analytical craftmanship at scale, with tremendous benefits both for the consumer and the economy. There are also new infrastructure companies that specifically emerged to support the data-driven economy that are growing faster than traditional infrastructure companies.

Finally, this book is intended to provide a framework and examples on how to think about data-driven business models so that you can create your own. Unlike the physical world, the digital world provides endless variations and opportunities to derive new business models or adjacent business models without cannibalizing those prior models. Data-driven business models disrupt and cannibalize only the traditional physical world business models. At the same time, they offer tremendous opportunities to build synergies with existing data-driven business models, which have multiplicative effect on the creation of value through the use of data.

We hope this book will inspire you and give you some ideas on how to build a new data-driven model or transition a traditional model to the new reality of the digital economy.

CHAPTER 2

Why Companies Miss Out on Big Opportunities

A few years ago, I visited a transportation company that also offered limo services to companies and business travelers. It had a substantial number of corporate accounts. As we walked to the conference room, I asked the CEO if he was worried about Uber. Uber had just reached over $1 billion valuation and was quickly becoming as trendy to use in the corporate world as it was to have a BlackBerry 10 years ago. After its launch, Black-Berry quickly became a status symbol of power and rank in the corporate hierarchy. After its fast ascent to a digital unicorn, using Uber became a symbol of being a young, modern, techno-trendy, and raising executives. Ditch the black car for the eye-catchy app that can hail a "cab" from anywhere.

My host stopped in the middle of the hallway, paused for a second, and said, "This is the wrong question. If CEOs in my position, who find themselves unexpectedly competing with Uber or another fast raising techno giant, are asking themselves this question, they are going to lose this battle." Then he turned and started walking in a different direction asking me to follow him and see him prove his point.

He opened a secured door and led me into a room full of people each staring at two, three, and even more monitors. They all had their phone headsets on. Multiple phone conversations were going on at the same time. I quickly realized that they were staring at maps on their computer screens. It was the dispatch room.

"This is our high-tech dispatch room," my host said as he led me closer to one of the desks. He leaned toward the screen and pointed at the screen where a bunch of little dots were moving on a map.

"Why didn't we invent Uber?" he asked me. "This is the right question! This is the question my board and my shareholders ask me because we had all the technology but failed to create Uber and increase the value of our company."

The room, the screens with the maps and the moving cars, the iPhones that could be seen on every desk, and the thought of the enormous Uber valuation made it immediately clear to me that this is the most painful question for every CEO who finds themselves in such a position. The company had all the technology but instead of building a self-service app, it continued to dispatch cars in the old-fashioned way—based on direct phone calls. All the employees had smartphones. All of them used apps on a regular basis to do various things. Why didn't it occur to any one of them to connect the drivers and the customers via an app? Despite their personal habits to use convenient self-service apps, no one clicked to convert their traditional phone-based personal service to an app-based self-service. Had they done so, they would have created enormous value for their shareholders. And this is precisely why the board and the shareholders were asking the CEO this question—why didn't we do it?

The CEO was asking the right question because it forces him and his executive team to understand and fix the underlying causes in the organization, its culture, and its processes that made them miss on an obvious opportunity. The gap between what they offered and the changing customer preferences for digital self-service ultimately opened the door for the entrance of a new and powerful competitor, which weakened the company's position in the marketplace.

This is not an isolated case. There are many companies who sell their data to start-ups, who within a few months sell them back a smart app to help their managers improve the businesses. They have sold an undervalued asset—the data—to another company that understood its value and came up with a business model to monetize this asset. From a shareholder perspective this is underutilization of assets and a transfer of value due to lack of ideas and knowledge about the new digital economy, where data-driven business models generate revenues.

The transition to the digital economy has changed the game rules and those who miss out on opportunities, because they do not understand how to create value with data, are shaken by the speed at which new entrants gobble their market share and dwarf their capitalizations.

And the reality is that more and more CEOs and executives will be held accountable for missing out on such opportunities.

Why Companies Miss on Opportunities

There are three reasons why companies miss on digital opportunities. And they are cultural.

First, companies do not see data as an asset. Second, companies do not know how to innovate with data. Third, companies do not think about data monetization, that is, they do not know how to build data products and data-driven business models.

Companies remain stuck in their familiar ways of managing assets and doing business while the times are changing. Economists call this phenomenon path dependency. The phenomenon was discovered when economists tried to understand why some progressive societies begin to decline and ultimately lose their economic advantages. The reason is quite simple. Deeply rooted traditions and norms force the younger generations to walk the same path while life demands change and adaptation. The path dependency prevents the progressive generation from moving forward. Institutions fail to change, and economic decline becomes permanent. The same holds true of companies.

The science of management has been developed in the last 100 years. The first MBA program was offered in Harvard Business School in 1908. For the past 100 years business education has been all about managing physical, financial, and human resources. How to manage data and digital assets has not been and is not taught at business schools. The business models of physical assets management are well studied and clearly explained. How to run a hospitality business and how to build a chain of hotels is textbook material. If you have the resources, you can follow the book and do it. But does any textbook mention how to build an Airbnb? No. This is because science follows practice. Hence, until a new business model is born in the real world, there are no references nor teaching materials about it.

Because in business, science follows practice and not the other way around, as it happens in other disciplines like medicine for example; many business scholars advocate the case method of teaching business. In other words, the aspiring business students learn by reading the historical cases of how businesses were created and managed. But in a fast-changing environment, managers who rely on book knowledge are at a disadvantage. It will take 20 to 30 years before we collect and synthesize the cases for data-driven business models and teach them at school the same way we teach finance and human resource. Managers can only learn by observing the reality and by letting the external cultural changes permeate their own organizational cultures. Managers must be observant and learn from theirs and other peoples' iPhone experiences about self-service, instead of holding to the landline to deliver on demand limo services to clients.

Let us look at the three cultural impediments to change.

Data Is Not Seen as an Asset

There is a lot of talk about data being an asset, but this is still lip service. If data was indeed seen as an asset it would have been already listed on the balance sheet. In fact, Doug Laney, a renowned industry analyst from Gartner, has coined the term "Infonomics"[1] as the practice of information economics. He is actively promoting the idea of putting data on the balance sheet and developing methodologies for accountants to measure its value and return on investment (ROI). Indeed, once anything becomes part of a balance sheet, it gets the full attention of auditors and stockholders, which in turn will ensure that data will be properly managed as an asset. Today this is not happening.

A Cambridge University[2] research survey reveals the top three reasons why data is not seen as an asset:

- First, 100 percent of the respondents to the survey agreed that they are experiencing cultural issues when trying to transition to data-driven business models.

---

[1] Infonomics https://gartner.com/en/publications/infonomics

[2] Brownlow, J., M. Zaki, A. Neely, and F. Urmetzer. 2015. "Data and Analytics—Data-Driven Business Models: A Blueprint for Innovation". *PDF File*, https://cambridgeservicealliance.eng.cam.ac.uk/resources/Downloads/Monthly%20Papers/2015MarchPaperTheDDBMInnovationBlueprint.pdf (accessed on November 12, 2019).

- Second, 86 percent of respondents agreed that there is a value perception that has impeded such implementation.
- Third, 71 percent of respondents agreed that there are data quality and integrity issues that make it difficult or impossible to implement a data-driven business model, as users quickly abandon apps that provide incorrect information.

We can clearly see in this triage that the adherence to old cultural practices drives the low value perception. It is also quite clear that data-related projects are not properly resourced because they are seen as less valuable to business. All the respondents stated that they lack expert resources to manage the data assets properly and improve its poor quality and integrity. But even worse, because data is not being seen as a valuable asset, people can be mocked for proposing ideas for making money with data. As we know from many historical examples, cultures can be quite brutal to the proponents of new ideas even when the cost of trial is practically zero. The Hungarian doctor Ignaz Semmelweis angered the entire medical community for advocating in the 1800s that doctors should wash their hands in chlorinated lime water before examining women about to deliver babies in order to reduce infection-related deaths. It took decades before Ignaz's practice became a norm in all hospitals because of the prevailing culture in the medical community. Many physicians were outraged at the thought that they might be the cause of death. Pride and dignity prevented them from trying a really low-cost solution with no potential drawbacks for trying it.

Unfortunately, the fact that many practices change only after a great resistance permeates the business world, too, and often impedes the creation of data-driven business models. The cost to business, employees, and shareholders is not as high as the social cost of the resistance to Ignaz's methods, but it is nevertheless significant. The fortunate situation in business is that while culture takes longer to change, value perceptions can change quickly based on market success and drive faster cultural change. To do that, businesses have to reward ideation and innovation with data.

Innovate With Data

Have you seen a company having a "Data R&D" department?

R&D is still tied to physical goods innovations—new chemical compounds, new gadgets, new drinks, new food ingredients, new food production, new packaging, new technologies, and so on. The list is endless. And, in fact, this innovation has been accelerated as we see new goods being introduced all the time. This rapid innovation has both positive and negative effects. Among the negative effects is accelerated consumerism. We all like novelty items, but because we are bombarded with new products the appreciation of the novelty is short lived. People experience user fatigue with gadgets, phones, and even big items like cars. Consumers have been conditioned to upgrade on a more or less regular schedule.

The accelerated innovation has become possible because of data and analytics. I recently visited FirstBuild (firstbuild.com), which pioneered a community-driven approach to innovation. The company is backed by GE appliances and is essentially an open co-working space for everyone who wants to innovate and build interesting and useful home appliances. As they say: "Think of it as a playground for adults. Our microfactory is a collaborative makerspace where ideas come to life. Use our tools and create your next big idea."[3] They have invented a number of useful products of which the most popular are the nugget ice maker for people who like chewable ice or slushy drinks, and the big clear ice balls maker for whiskey lovers who like their drink to be chilled without being watered down.

I was most impressed by how they used sensors and data to create the perfect pizza oven for the home. As they explained it is really hard to make a good pizza because restaurant grade brick ovens heat the stone up to 800°F (427°C) and the dome up to 1300°F (704°C), which distributed the heat perfectly around the pizza. This is an extremely high and dangerous temperature for a residential home. Hence, the engineers at FirstBuild had to come up with many technical innovations to make such an appliance safe for the home.

But what was most interesting is how they determined the method to distribute the temperature in order to make the best pizza. They installed over 1,000 heat resistant sensors in the best pizza restaurants and collected

---

[3] Learn More About First Build. https://firstbuild.com/about/ (accessed on November 23, 2019).

data on the heat distribution inside the brick ovens. Based on the data, they came up with precise four-zone temperature controls, which ensure that exact temperatures are hit and maintained every single time. The miniaturization of the brick oven for home use was made possible because of the combination of engineering and data analytics techniques.

Today, research shows that putting a data scientist on the innovation team can increase productivity significantly. Traditionally the optimal heat points would have been found by trial and error. Data analysis reduces the experimentation time required to arrive at the optimal solution.

It is great that "hot" data helped create the best home pizza oven. But can the oven help make new products? The answer is yes. Today, all kinds of products have collected data that provides valuable information on usage and operating patterns. Insights about the operating patterns lead to feature and function improvements, while insights about the usage patterns lead to new product ideas. A research paper on the Future of R&D[4] points out that companies like "Caterpillar, Rolls Royce Aerospace, and Tesla are using Big Data generated from sensors to plan their next product improvements and to determine what features and components need to be enhanced or created." The impact of pattern analysis is even greater in health care. Big multidimensional and granular data can reveal previously unknown microtrends which lead to more effective, personalized treatments.

So, why do we need a data R&D department? The current R&D is goal oriented and not exploratory. In other words, innovators first come with a vision and then pursue its implementation. Data turns this approach upside down. Granular data (such as sensor data for example) is like DNA. It already contains all the important information. All that remains to be done is to dig out the insights and hand them to the traditional R&D department to create new products and services.

---

[4] Jeffrey, A., (SRI International) M. Blackburn (Cargill), and D. Legan (Kraft Foods) "Big Data and the Future of R&D Management." http://iriweb.org/sites/default/files/Big%20Data%20Primer.pdf (accessed on November 18, 2019).

Monetize Your Data Assets

The first large-scale data projects aiming to extract value and insights from data were the data warehouses. Companies started to develop their own custom data warehouses in 1980 in order to transform data collected from operations into data ready for analytics and reporting. These data warehouses became the foundation of "Business Intelligence"—a term coined by the Gartner analyst Howard Dresner[5] to describe the use of databases, datamarts, query and analysis technologies to provide decision makers with timely, factual, information. Making better decisions makes the business more intelligent.

Three years ago, I met the head of the innovation lab of Walmart, who was a veteran Business Intelligence specialist. He had started his career at Procter and Gamble's diapers business. His first assignment was to develop and present statistical reports on the diaper business to the founder and CEO of Walmart—one of their largest retailers. At the time it took him six months to extract shipment and other data and build reports against the Unix system. At the meeting with Sam Walton he presented detailed information on all shipments to all states and all stores. After the review of the numbers, Sam Walton seemed unimpressed despite the wealth of very detailed information. He told the young analyst that he had not answered the most important question that every CEO and every manager should know at the end of every day: "Did we make money?"

It took the analyst another six months to collect the data and answer this question. At the follow-up meeting he told Sam Walton and the present Walmart executives that they had lost money. Seemingly unsurprised, Sam Walton made a point to his executives. If they knew the financial results at the close of business every day, they could manage and turn the loss into profit. But if the losses are revealed a year later, they would go out of business. That, according to my host, led to the creation of Retail

---

[5] "In 1989, Howard Dresner (later a Gartner analyst) proposed business intelligence as an umbrella term to describe 'concepts and methods to improve business decision making by using fact-based support systems.' It was not until the late 1990s that this usage was widespread." https://en.wikipedia.org/wiki/Business_intelligence (accessed on December 14, 2019).

Link—the famous system that provided important profit and loss information to both merchandisers and suppliers. In turn, this system allowed for the development and execution of the famous "Always Low Prices" strategy.

The data warehouse still plays an important role in business. But it is interesting that no data warehouse project ever starts with the objective to monetize the data in it. Data warehouses were justified as a means to better and more timely reporting. They supported other activities and had no direct role in the making of money. Hence, they were a cost center in the organizations. Why is this wrong?

In the traditional school of management, we cannot even imagine a manager who would propose a new investment without calculating its ROI. But the ROI on a data warehouse built to support better decisions is impossible to quantify. Who can collect information on how decisions are made? And who can calculate the incremental improvement achieved with one decision versus another? Two store managers can make two different decisions based on the same report, but the financial outcomes may be the same. If data is converted to product, the ROI on it can be quantified in the same way as we do for physical goods.

The reality is that a data warehouse can be used both for decision support and for data monetization. The two are not mutually exclusive. The beauty of data is that once it is collected and properly managed as an asset it can be used for multiple purposes. Data is a true "renewable resource." By adopting a data monetization mindset, companies will start leveraging data more actively as a limitless resource that can routinely produce new revenue streams.

Adopting a New Mindset

A "data first" approach to business requires a deep cultural change, which is never easy. But does it have to be that difficult? Cultural change in organizations follows market success. Seeing more success stories about making money with data stimulates employees to be curious and motivates them to learn. Ultimately, the organization transitions from path dependency to trend following, which changes the value perception of data-related products or business models.

Since making data products is much cheaper than making physical products, it pays to encourage intrapreneurship with data. Some of the most effective data products have started as skunk work but have transformed the fortunes and cultures in their companies. The most famous and widely discussed example of such a skunk data project is the invention of the connection suggestions on LinkedIn. This data product led to the launch of the "data scientists" as "the sexiest job of the 21st century."[6]

---

[6] Davenport, T.H., and D.J. Patil. 2012. "Data Scientist: The Sexiest Job of the 21st Century." *Harvard Business Review*.

CHAPTER 3

Everything Is Changing

There are times in history when new technologies emerge and change how we do everything:

- How we do our jobs,
- How we do business, and
- How we compete in the marketplace.

The steam engine is one such technology. It created the modern factory and changed how people worked. It also opened new markets due to new distribution capabilities that created new multinational conglomerates. Since companies were not constrained anymore to their local markets, they grew internationally.

The microscope is another piece of technology with a profound social and economic effect. It allowed researchers and medical professionals to see things that they could not see with their eyes, leading to the discovery of new targets for treatments. In turn, this created an enormous supply of new treatments and big pharma. Today companies are building even larger microscopes in search of more targets at a more granular level. As the lead researcher on the development of an extremely large microscope at University of Strathclyde in Scotland says: "You are studying a world which doesn't even obey the same rules of perception."[1]

Big granular data, that is, data collected in milliseconds, seconds, and minutes, contains patterns, shapes, and trends that cannot be seen by the human eye. But when algorithms reveal to business professionals the insights contained in the raw data, it becomes a source of new data-driven

---

[1] Laura, P. 2017. "Let Us Now Praise the Invention of the Microscope." https://smithsonianmag.com/science-nature/what-we-owe-to-the-invention-microscope-180962725/ (accessed on November 12, 2019).

products and data-driven business models. It creates a supply of new goods and services delivered by new digital giants.

How can data be the raw material for such growth?

Let's Eliminate Heart-Related Sudden Deaths

Do you know that 50 percent of sudden deaths are caused by heart related conditions? And 80 percent of them are preventable …

—said Ivo Datchov, the CEO of a small startup, Check Point Cardio (checkpointcardio.com).

He then handed me a newspaper clip from the Bulgarian press.[2] It told the story of a 61-year-old person with a heart condition who experienced a medical condition while waiting to board a plane.

"This condition occurs for 3–4 minutes and the patient may be completely unaware of it. If the symptoms are not caught in time, it leads to certain death."

Fortunately for the patient, he was wearing one of Check Point Cardio's remote monitoring devices. The device detected the symptoms in real time, sent the patient's ECG and other vitals to the data center, and alerted the personnel at the remote diagnostic center about the medical emergency. A physician reviewed the data streams from the device, assigned a diagnosis, and called the patient to instruct him what to do until he was picked by an ambulance 30 minutes later.

Ivo explained to me that the company was founded because of a very passionate cardiologist working in a hospital in Kazanlak—a small town located at the east end of the Rose Valley in Bulgaria. During his tenure the cardiologist observed that many cardio-related deaths occur after patients are discharged from the hospital, return to their natural living environments, and resume their normal daily routines. In many cases the patients do not even feel the symptoms of deteriorating conditions, and thus, they cannot seek help from their physician. If patients could be monitored remotely for the occurrence of adverse symptoms, and if the

---

[2] https://24chasa.bg/zdrave/article/6601711 (accessed November 23, 2019).

changes in the patient's condition could be communicated immediately to a cardiologist specialist, many deaths would become preventable.

As Yuval Harari points in his futuristic book "Homo Deus,"[3] because of technological advances many deaths today are viewed as technical error. Cars do not have the right equipment to prevent deaths, patients are not equipped with the right monitoring devices, and many more. The team behind Check Point Cardio thought in the same way. The limitation was in the monitoring technology and not in the treatment. They knew that a practical solution required patients to be monitored 24/7 in their natural environments. If patients are kept in the hospital too long, the cost is too high. If they were discharged without remote monitoring, they were at risk. Thus, sudden cardio-related death is a technical problem.

Check Point Cardio's first device was a 140-gram wearable monitor. It monitors 12 channels of ECG, pulse, blood pressure, respiratory activity and the bodily movements of the patient. The device tracks every movement of the patient and his or her exact location in case of emergency. Monitoring all these vitals simultaneously provides enough information for hospital-grade clinical diagnosis. For example, the correlation between blood pressure and ECG measurements produces very reliable signals for detecting many deteriorating heart conditions.

Many interesting innovations are packed in this tiny device. The ability to measure the blood pressure of a patient in motion in real time without a cuff is an impressive achievement. It is impossible to measure blood pressure with a cuff while someone is running or sleeping. The team guards the secret about how they do the blood pressure measurements as tightly as the Coca-Cola formula is being guarded. Equally important and impressive is what they do with the data.

The device collects 250 measurements per second. This is 15,000 data points per minute per measure, 900,000 per hour per measure, and 21,600,000 points per day per measure. To put this into perspective, an

---

[3] Yuval, H. 2017. *Homo Deus: A Brief History of Tomorrow*. HarperCollins.

Excel can analyze only one hour of this data as Excel can load up to 1 million data points. The data packets collected every second have to be sent over the Internet to remote monitoring centers without any loss of information. Any loss of information makes the diagnosis more difficult or impossible. The human body produces a lot of noise that clutters the signal and makes diagnosis more difficult. A body in motion produces even more noise and thus makes remote monitoring in natural environments more challenging. It is the data scientists who use specialized algorithms to surgically remove the bodily noise from the data. Finally, the data is visualized and algorithmically annotated to direct the physician immediately to the most relevant segments in this enormous time series sequence. A three-minute symptom generates a long time series sequence of 45,000 points that is hard to explore with the naked eye. But machines and algorithms can explore every detail of sequences of any lengths and augment the human eye in the detection of medical pathologies in the same way the microscope does in the detection of targets.

Check Point Cardio's vision is not just prevention but also better health care for patients. Living in your natural environment risk-free is better than living safe in a hospital. This improvement in patient care is obvious, but what is less obvious is how such technology and data change the business of health care.

Jobs Are Changing

Technologies like Check Point Cardio's remote monitor fundamentally change how physicians do their jobs. In traditional health care the patient is examined physically by the doctor. Both the patient and the physician are in the same room. Even if some monitoring equipment, such as a stationary ECG recorder, is used, the exam is confined to a physical location and a specific time frame. This is no longer the case. The patient can be anywhere—at work, at home, on the road, and so on.

The fact that the patient is not confined for examination and treatment to a physical location has enormous social and economic benefits. People can return to work faster and be cared for at their homes, which saves hospital and other costs, and provides emotional support. But it changes the relationship between the patient and the doctor.

First, doctors are used to examining and diagnosing patients in person. They ask questions, perform physical exams, feel how the patient feels, and make judgments based on the soft signals that they get from patients. Sensing soft cues during an in-person medical exam is what physicians rely on to ensure that the diagnosis is accurate and that they have not missed important signs of other conditions.

In the future remote health monitoring will reduce the need for physical exams. The missing soft cues that aid the physician's intuition during a physical exam will be replaced by granular data on vital signals and symptoms. Instead of guessing from cues, data collected at 250 milliseconds will provide the doctor with a much more factual picture of the person's health and medical conditions. Unlike the human brain, algorithms can sift through tremendous volumes of information to ensure that all possibilities are accurately assessed and considered. Consequently, physicians will have to hone different skills. Instead of developing a sense for soft cues from patients, they will develop skills to sift through data and analytics quickly to diagnose and treat patients remotely. It must be noted that *intuition is a practical guide to decision making only in the absence of complete information.* Today's monitoring systems are evolving quickly to collect ubiquitously all the data required to make decisions.

Second, the patient/doctor relationship will change because it will no longer be structured based on periodic scheduled visits. Because of the 24/7 real-time monitoring, the relationship becomes continuous. The doctor is now available on demand 24/7 because the remote monitoring device can alert them at any time about changes in the patient's health conditions. The transition from scheduled visits to on-as-needed care improves the outcomes, saves time, and ultimately allows physicians to deliver care to far more patients.

In this section I used the example of remote health monitoring to illustrate how technology and data change the medical profession. But data-driven devices and processes will change every job in a similar way. The new condition-based maintenance (CBM) models for industrial equipment are conceptually the same as the remote health care model. CBM allows companies to transition from scheduled maintenance to conditioned-based as-needed maintenance to save time and costs.

The fundamental job changes come for two reasons. First, decision makers will not have to be present at the action site in order to make decisions and change the outcomes. Like doctors, factory managers, mining managers, and many more engineers can control the outcomes in their production processes remotely. Second, decision makers will not be forced to make judgment calls on incomplete information. Their expert knowledge will be augmented with granular data analytics similarly to how we use other tools to aid our activities.

Business Models Are Changing

Insurance companies typically reimburse doctors, hospitals, and other patient care centers for patient visits and hospital stays. Doctors and nurses are also reimbursed for any in-person visits to patients at their homes. These are a pay-per-visit and pay-for-stay business models.

My first experience with remote medical care was 15 years ago when my daughter was growing. Our pediatrician often gave us advice over the phone in order to save us a trip to his office. When I called to schedule a visit, I often could hear him asking his nurse: "Ask them what it is about?" If it turned out to be something small and trivial, he would grab the phone and tell me: "Why waste an hour in traffic when I can tell you exactly what to do now?" I always appreciated him saving me the trip, especially after long office hours and during weekends. But he never got paid for his remote advice. It did not matter how much time he spent on the phone or how many calls he got from me about the same issue. At the time insurers did not consider such remote guidance to be true medical care, even though our doctor cared both for my daughter's health and for my convenience and time. As the times are changing, some insurance companies are starting to pay for phone and e-mail medical advice, but it is still not the norm.[4]

----

[4] "In the past, discussing medical issues and getting medical advice over the phone was not reimbursed by insurance or billed to patients. Recently, some private insurance companies have begun to pay for patient-to-provider phone calls, especially when the calls are prolonged and when medical decisions are made. Nevertheless, you may be billed for the whole cost, or you may have to pay a co-pay." https://verywellhealth.com/cpt-and-hcpcs-codes-for-telephone-calls-and-emails-2615304 (accessed on November 23, 2019).

The remote monitoring technology changes the pay-per-visit model to a subscription model as service is being provided continuously. The patient pays the subscription for as long as he or she is being monitored. The pay-per-visit model is discontinuous and, thus, has many drawbacks. Most importantly there are information gaps between the different visits. What has happened in-between is anecdotal. The information provided to the physician is whatever the patient remembers or wants to tell the doctor. Many conditions remain unnoticed, too, as they can only be detected with sophisticated equipment. Those gaps of information are the most common cause of deteriorating medical conditions and even sudden death.

The subscription model delivers uninterrupted continuity of service. When continuity is built into the business model everything becomes easier and predictable—the care, the business revenues, the planning for resources, and much more. Sensors and other data collection technologies allow for the building of data-driven business models based on continuous service. There are many other data-driven business models that rely on a continuous supply of information but the service itself is not continuous. The short-term rental business model pioneered by Airbnb relies on a continuous supply of information about the available properties, the quality of the individual properties, the prudence of the renters to ensure trust in the supply and demand network, and so on. Because data can be used in many ways, it presents an opportunity to create many different data-driven business models. In this sense the analogy that "data is the new crude oil" is true. There are over 150 different products made of petroleum and the list keeps growing as new inventions are created.[5] The list of data products is even larger and is growing at a faster rate.

Market Competition Is Changing

The ability to provide reliable, uninterrupted, real-time care remotely allows companies to create remote monitoring and diagnostic franchises.

---

[5] Chisolm, K. 2019. "144 Products Made From Petroleum And 4 That May Shock You." *Innovative Advisory Group,* https://innovativewealth.com/inflation-monitor/what-products-made-from-petroleum-outside-of-gasoline/

These franchises can take care of a lot more patients than hospitals can. They can be located anywhere and even outsource to low cost countries. Essentially, the technology makes it possible to outsource components of medical care in the same way as other technologies have made it possible to outsource customer service and call centers.

For certain services we place higher value on the in-person versus remote service. This has been especially true of health care. However, the attitudes are changing. The health care system is overloaded and under-staffed. People hate the long waiting time in hospitals and physicians' offices. They also hate to be restricted about where and how they get service. People value their time and mobility more than the in-personal service and this will drive the wide acceptance of remote care. At the end of the day, a visit to a hospital is not a social engagement, it is a need and if the trip can be saved without compromising the quality of the service, both the patient and the physician will be better off.

The competition is changing because the remote franchises will put enormous competitive pressure on traditional hospitals and health service providers. These new business models compete directly with the tradi-tional providers for patients and revenues. As the cost of remote monitor-ing continues to drop, the franchises will start competing with the family doctors for the delivery of routine health checks. Companies like Check Point Cardio are working to embed sensors in undershirts, so that even healthy people can be monitored 24/7. Such wearable devices will turn the current way of scheduling doctor's appointments upside down. People will not go to the doctor when they feel discomfort. They will be called with a diagnosis and treatment prescription even when they do not feel any symptoms.

Technology always has an impact on the market competition as it gives companies a competitive advantage. Car manufacturers are con-stantly innovating to gain competitive advantage and market share from their rivals. Building a better mouse trap is a strategy to temporarily out-perform your competitors. It is like playing tit-for-tat. If Ford has a better model today, next season GM will release the new newsmaker model. But when new technologies facilitate the creation of new business models, the competition is not about building a better mouse trap; it is about build-ing better institutions that make the old institutions obsolete.

Adaptation Is Survival

When new business models disrupt the institutional structure of the market, change and adaptation are the only viable strategies. The resistance to change during times of high disruption is because many managers see the new market competition as a zero-sum game. The remote patient monitoring and diagnostic centers will be the winners and traditional hospitals and family doctors will be the losers. The new entrants are perceived just as low-cost providers that cannibalize the revenues of the traditional health care service providers.

This kind of thinking is a remnant of the old physical economy mindset. If resources are limited and finite, the ownership and control of resources is a zero-sum game. If we change the focal point, we can see that continuous 24/7 monitoring provides more opportunities for more diversified services. As it extends from patients to healthy individuals, it in fact increases the market for health care services dramatically. Instead of less, all participants in the health care industry end up with more opportunities. It is just a matter of plugging all organizations into the data stream so new opportunities and services can be developed faster. And the biggest winner of this data-driven ecosystem are the patients who are saved from sudden deaths.

CHAPTER 4

Scale and Scope in the Digital Economy

On March 19, 2019, the APNews published a story about the last remaining species of its kind in Oregon. But it is not a biological species going extinct. Oregon's Blockbuster retail store became the last on Earth when the only other store in Perth, Australia closed its doors on March 31, 2019.[1]

The store systems and operation are so archaic that one wonders how it could function:

> The computer system must be rebooted using floppy disks that only the general manager ... knows how to use. The dot-matrix printer broke, so employees write out membership cards by hand. And the store's business transactions are backed up on a reel-to-reel tape that can't be replaced because Radio Shack went out of business. Everything in this store is a technological oldie—the systems, the video tapes and CDs, the service. And this is precisely why it survives and thrives.

In 2004, Blockbuster had 9,000 high-end, high-tech stores globally. In 2014, it closed all company-owned stores. A few franchised stores remain in business primarily as tourist attractions—remnants of a vanished retail empire and obsolete technologies. The store is a symbol of the new market competition in which many companies and technologies go from raise to demise quickly. The Oregon store now sells T-shirts, caps, and other goods with their own branding "The Last Blockbuster in America," and they seem to fly off the shelves.

---

[1] Flaccus, G. 2019. "Oregon Blockbuster Outlasts Others to Become Last on Earth." *AP News,* https://apnews.com/e543db5476c749038435279edf2fd60f (accessed November 12, 2019).

Many people attribute the failure of Blockbuster to Netflix—the company that flipped the in-store model to mail-in self-service. But it is more complex than that. If you think about it, why didn't Blockbuster buy Netflix or build a competitive mail-in offering? It didn't for a long time, and when it did it was too late. This is because of path dependency.

The Blockbuster business model and revenues critically depended on the collection of late charges.[2] Late charges are a penalty that the customers pay for returning the rented movie to the physical store past its due date. I paid a lot of late fees myself. I would say that I probably paid late fees on 60 percent of my rentals. I hated the late fees because in most cases there were some extraneous circumstances that did not allow me to drive to the store and return the movies on time. If the store was more conveniently located, or if there was another easier way to return the movies, I would have done it. Hence, I did not consider it my fault for being late and the penalty seemed unjust. But Blockbuster was too attached to collecting penalties from its customers and did not want to give up the easy revenue. They knew very well that a subscription-based business model would eliminate the penalties and drain their key revenue source.

But why didn't they see the emerging subscription model by Netflix as a threat that could cannibalize their rental revenues?

The reason why they did not see the mail-in subscription as a threat is because of what I call the illusion of assets advantage. The Blockbuster executives felt secure behind their massive network of 9,000 physical stores. Coming from the world of physical assets, this network was their highest managerial achievement. At that time, most retailers viewed such asset accumulation as a means to put a Chinese wall around their customers. The more stores they had, the more customer visits they expected.[3] Thus, in a classical path dependent thinking, the Blockbuster executives

---

[2] Forbes. 2014. "A Look Back At Why Blockbuster Really Failed And Why It Didn't Have To." *Forbers,* https://forbes.com/sites/gregsatell/2014/09/05/a-look-back-at-why-blockbuster-really-failed-and-why-it-didnt-have-to/#1edf39a61d64 (accessed November 12, 2019).

[3] The Canadian clothing retailer Zellers failed too because their Chinese wall thinking. They embarked on a strategy to acquire more locations as a means to get more customers. The cost of those stores ultimately took them out of business.

could not comprehend that the asset-based competitive advantage could evaporate quickly. A competitor without assets was perceived as a soldier without weapons—not a great threat. Well-established managerial traditions, practices, and pride got in the way of seeing the new reality. The asset, that is, the physical store, was the cause of the inconvenience to consumers, and the inconvenience was the source of the late penalty revenue stream. Netflix eliminated the asset and built a new asset-less retail model.

Eventually Blockbuster introduced mail-in self-service, but it was too late. The story of Blockbuster's failure is about how scale in the physical world works against you and how scale in the digital world works for you when competing against a traditional asset-based business. Once the asset-less movie rental model was adopted and consumers started to reduce or abandoned store visits altogether, the ownership and management of physical stores became a cost-drag for Blockbuster.

Scale and Scope in the Traditional Economy

Economists like to measure growth in terms of scale and scope. Scale is how fast companies go from small to large, that is, large volumes of production, a large network of stores, hotels, and so on. Scale correlates with market share because companies need scale to meet customer demand. In the world of physical resources scale implies investment in physical assets. Thus, in the traditional physical economy, scale gave the owners of assets a reliable protection against new entrants.

In 2016, Tesla made a bold statement that it would increase the production of its Model 3 electric car to 500,000 units by 2020. Many logistics experts were skeptical about this goal because Tesla did not have experience with mass production.[4] Scaling the production to such magnitude for a product that comprises more than 10,000 individual parts is the know-how and expertise of companies that have over 100

---

[4] Supply Chain Game Changer. 2019. "Drawing Lessons From Tesla's Supply Chain Issues!" https://supplychaingamechanger.com/drawing-lessons-from-teslas-supply-chain-issues/ (accessed November 12, 2019).

years history in car manufacturing. Tesla lacked not only the experience but also the ability to hire all the needed talent to achieve this goal. As expected, it failed to produce the 500,000 cars and meet the expectations of thousands of consumers who had signed up on a waiting list for the Model 3 Tesla. The car manufacturers in Detroit indeed had a competitive advantage secured by the known challenges in scaling the production of physical goods. Despite all the hype in the press about the Tesla creative destruction of Detroit car manufacturing, the Big Three kept their cool and waited to become fast-second in the newly emerging category of electric cars. Fast-second companies do not partake in the risk of market development, but they can only succeed if they have enough time to catch up. As it can be seen from this example, fast-second is a strategy that works in the traditional market competition. In 2019, all the Big Three announced rollouts of their own brands of electric cars, which is beginning to negatively impact the demand and market leadership of Tesla.

Scope is the ability to expand the existing business into new product categories within the same market or into adjacent markets. In the automotive market, there are many categories—sedans, sports cars, SUVs, trucks, luxury cars, and many more. Inventing a new category, as Chrysler did when they introduced the minivan, is a sure way to expand market share. As the market gets consolidated, the big players play in all categories, as it is easy for them to leverage their scale to expand their scope. Niche players who try to dominate one category get acquired as it happened to Rolls-Royce and Porsche.[5] This is the reason why Tesla entered multiple categories—sports, sedan, and SUV. Since in the physical world scope is ensured through resources and capacity, it also serves as protection against new entrants.

But do scale and scope effects work in the same way in the digital economy?

---

[5] More information on the lessons learned from the history of niche players in the automotive history can be found here: "A Dangerous Time to Be a Niche Player" https://atkearney.com/strategy-and-top-line-transformation/article?/a/a-dangerous-time-to-be-a-niche-player (accessed November 12, 2019).

Scale and Scope in the Digital Economy

Traditionally it took companies 15 or more years to reach $1 billion market valuation. Uber reached $3.7 billion valuation in 36 months (October 2010 to August 2013[6]) and there is a growing number of companies who achieve it in two years on average. The main reason for Uber's fast-paced growth is that its data-driven business model is not constrained by the accumulation of physical assets. The cars were already available; they just had to be mobilized and put into a money-making service. The growth of Uber can only be limited by their ability to manage the data about the cars, the drivers, and the riders, which requires far less resources than managing and maintaining cars, employing and managing drivers.

The importance of collecting and managing all aspects of the data related to the service can best be illustrated by reviewing the impact that criminal or abusive actions have on the business. Just a small number of criminal actions by a few drivers can seriously impact the trust in Uber and the demand for its services. Not having the right data to stop and prevent such offences is a bigger danger to Uber than the lack or loss of a physical asset. There is a constant supply of Uber cars that come with the drivers, but the reputational damage of a single incident drastically affects consumer demand. Criminal incidents happen in company-owned cabs too, but somehow there was a false belief that employing drivers ensures higher scrutiny than managing a decentralized group of freelance drivers.

As Benjamin Franklin said: "It takes many good deeds to build a good reputation, and only one bad one to lose it."[7] And while there are not many companies that go bankrupt for reputational damage, they pay a significant cost to recover fleeing customers. Thus, the scaling of Uber is contingent only on the trust in the quality of its service, which the data management system makes 100 percent transparent for every driver and

---

[6] Olsen, D. 2017. "Uber by the Numbers: A Timeline of the Company's Funding and Valuation History." *Pitchbook,* https://pitchbook.com/news/articles/uber-by-the-numbers-a-timeline-of-the-companys-funding-and-valuation-history (accessed November 12, 2019).

[7] Eccles, R.G., S.C. Newquist, and R. Schatz. 2007. "Reputation and Its Risks." *Harvard Business Review* 85, no. 2, p. 104.

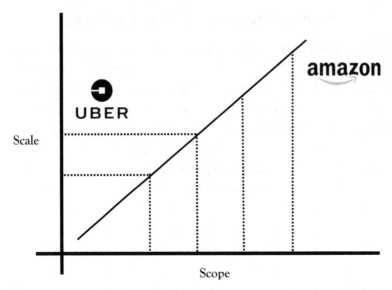

Figure 4.1 Growth through scale and scope expansion: A model for the digital economy

client. The transparency maintains the trust and ensures that customers can choose who to ride with and drivers can choose whom to pick up.

Amazon scaled its book selling business fast and then it started to expand its scope quickly to become one of the largest companies in the world. The effect of the scope expansion on Amazon's market cap is astonishing. It's market cap grew from $20 billion in 2008 when it embarked on a scope expansion to $950 billion in 2018. This is a 4,650 percent increase in value in 10 years. Scope expansion scales the market cap of digital companies (Figure 4.1).

Data-driven companies have an advantage when they expand their scope. They can apply the same data management know-how to new categories and new businesses. Whether you sell books, shoes, clothes, gadgets, appliances, or anything else, the sales process, the data management, and the analytics that drive the sales are the same. But unlike traditional companies, digital companies do not require capital investment in physical assets to monetize their know-how.

Even more interesting is how Amazon created their cloud services business AWS. AWS was developed in three years out of an internal need to make its sales process more flexible and powerful, as they were expanding the scale of the business to more merchants.[8] As management watched the use and operations of the new system, they realized that they had become real experts in managing data and infrastructure. Why not rent this capability to any other companies? Amazon was already renting space on their digital storefront to other retailers. Now they could rent infrastructure, too, not only to merchants who sell on Amazon but to any company in the world.

Thus, in just a few years through expansion in scale and scope Amazon has taken on two traditional giants in two different industries—Walmart and IBM. It is interesting that IBM was in the business of infrastructure management but never thought to build and sell it as a service, while Walmart had the Retail Link system but never thought to package it as a product and rent it to other vendors. Amazon had the thought-advantage to invent an entirely new business because of its continuous expansion through data management and analytics.

Digital Growth

In the new digital economy, scale is achieved not through the accumulation of assets but through mobilizing and onboarding customers on data-driven platforms and products. Scope is expanded not through investments in capacity and assets, but through the digitization of adjacent processes and services. Chat apps like WhatsApp, Telegram, KaKao Talk, WeChat, and so on used to be only for chat. But today they can be used to make calls, order cabs, pay bills, and much more. And why not? After all, we used to do these things by chatting in-person or on the phone to dispatchers, bank tellers, and other service providers.

---

[8] Miller, R. 2016. "How AWS Came to Be." *TechCrunch*. https://tech crunch.com/2016/07/02/andy-jassys-brief-history-of-the-genesis-of-aws/ (accessed November 12, 2019).

CHAPTER 5

The New Economics
of Disaggregation and Scale

Traditional economics is based on accumulation, aggregation, and concentration to create scale and market power. The Ford Model-T business model is about demand aggregation by offering a single, mass produced car model at a very low cost. Today, the manufacturing industry is moving in the opposite direction—away from uniform standardization for low cost mass production and toward mass customization at a scale achieved through deep analytics for product personalization. Adidas has pioneered a new analytical craftsmanship that allows for the mass production of ergonomically personalized sneakers that we will discuss in Part II of this book.

The Hilton hotel chain is an example of growth through the accumulation of assets. This model was turned upside down by the completely asset-less and massively successful short-term rental model of Airbnb. In the 1950s, the shopping mall model became very successful because it concentrated a large number of diverse shops into a single location. This made the shopping trip easier for consumers and simultaneously increased the share-of-wallet due to the larger variety of goods. Amazon successfully took the physical mall out of the business model to save consumers the entire trip and to gain even a larger share of the consumers' wallet.

All of these business models have produced large-scale operations that have captured significant market share in their industries. However, today the successful models from the physical economy are in tight competition with the new business models of the digital economy, and the economics of growth is radically different.

Disaggregation, Concentration, and Accumulation

Complete aggregation, that is, the ability to aggregate and capture the entire demand for particular goods and achieve a monopoly, is impossible in the physical world. Yet, it is quite possible in the digital world through the process of disaggregation. It is the fundamental reason for the fast growth of the digital giants.

No long ago I was discussing with Gerald Cohen, founder of Information Builders Inc., whether we can judge correctly the likelihood of success or failure of start-ups. We agreed that we place a great value on the business model, but even more so on the impression that the founder makes on us. And then Gerry said: "But even that can be quite misleading and quite difficult to judge."

He then told me how he met Jeff Bezos when he was just starting and pitching his early stage Amazon venture. Gartner Inc., the global research firm that provides insights and studies on emerging technology trends and technology management practices, organized regular lunches between CEOs of successful, established companies and newly founded start-ups. At one such event Gerry Cohen and Bill Gates had to share a table with two aspiring entrepreneurs. Both founders were selling goods online. The difference was that one was selling wine and the other books.

When the two founders left the table, Gerry and Bill started to discuss which one of the two had more chances to succeed. They both thought that the wine business had a bigger chance to succeed and were almost certain that the book business would fail.[1] They thought that the business models were the same and, hence, put more faith in the charming personality and storytelling of the wine seller. As we know today Gerry and Bill were wrong.

---

[1] Jeff Bezos himself told early investors that Amazon was likely to fail. In a recent interview he told employees: "Amazon is Not Too Big to Fail … In Fact, I Predict One Day Amazon Will Fail. Amazon Will Go Bankrupt. If You Look at Large Companies, Their Lifespans Tend to be 30-Plus Years, Not a Hundred-Plus Years." https://theguardian.com/technology/2018/nov/16/jeff-bezos-amazon-will-fail-recording-report (Perhaps the fear of failure drives the hard work to deliver success.)

It is interesting why, at the early stages of online retailing, selling books turned out to be more successful than selling any other type of product. Bezos gives the following two reasons why he chose books.[2] According to him books have a distinct retail advantage because they are sortable, packageable, and shippable. Second, there is an overwhelming number of already existing books that cannot be displayed and sold even in the largest brick-and-mortar bookstore. In other words, the demand for books cannot be completely aggregated as no retailer can sell all the books in the world. Furthermore, no retailer could even own copies of all the books existing in the world. But Amazon did not have these limitations. It did not need to own copies of the books either as it simply allowed people and organizations to sell second-hand books on its platform. In this way Amazon was able to expand its catalogue of books beyond anything that its brick-and-mortar competitors could do.

The supply and demand argument that Bezos emphasized could be made for any type of product. There are more bottles of wine in the world than any shop or liquor retailer can own, store, and sell. The markets for clothes, shoes, electronics, and so on all share the same limitations. Supply cannot meet all the demand in the world because of physical constraints.

On the other hand, Bezos' first reason about why he chose books cannot be made for many types of products. Wine is not easily sortable, packageable, and shippable. It is also hard to store. For many years the fear of shopping online was caused mainly by concerns about the delivery of the purchased goods. What would happen if the bottle of wine was broken during shipment, what if the shoes were not the right size, and what if the material of the dress was not as it appeared on the picture and in the description? Many successful online retailers had to build in their business models the means to ensure the trust of the consumer that the delivered goods would arrive and be of the quality that they expected at the point of purchase. Zappos' success of selling shoes online is largely attributed to the invention of the free returns which alleviated shoe shoppers of the fear of regret.

---

[2] Hunt, H. 2018. "First Mover: Jeff Bezos In His Own Words (In Their Own Words Series)." *Agate Publishing*.

It is either the stroke of a genius or pure luck that such fears did not exist for shipping books. The postal service has been delivering letters, papers, magazines, and books packaged in envelopes for many years. People are accustomed to receiving printed materials in the mail and know that there is minimal risk for damage during shipment. Because of this, consumers had no psychological barriers to shop for books online. On the contrary, they just could benefit from the large variety and lower prices. The pre-existing consumer trust in the new business model provided Amazon with easy access to early adopters and a staying power through the early stages of online retailing that ultimately allowed Amazon to expand into other product categories. Trusting Amazon for the delivery of books gradually led to trusting Amazon for the delivery of anything.

Amazon is an example of the ability to disaggregate demand to an extreme. As the merchandise catalog expanded, Amazon could satisfy more and more niche preferences. This has become known as long tail retailing. "Long tail" is a statistical concept about the distribution of events. Popular items have a higher frequency of occurrence than less popular items. In retail, more frequently purchased items tend to be easier to find. They are placed in more visible locations in the stores; there is more advertising of them, and more reviews. This was the fundamental idea behind the Ford Model-T. The lower the cost, the higher the frequency of purchase. The higher the frequency of purchasing the more awareness in the market as everyone sees and hears about the Model T. This leads to an always increasing frequency of purchase.

But there are a lot more products and untapped revenue opportunities in the long tail if a retailer can make special items with low frequencies of purchase as easily accessible as the high-frequency products. Some economists have estimated that the sales potential in the long tail is at least equal if not greater than that of high-frequency items. The economic theory of the long tail states that:

> Our culture and economy is increasingly shifting away from a focus on a relatively small number of "hits" (mainstream products and markets) at the head of the demand curve and toward a huge number of niches in the tail. As the costs of production and

distribution fall, especially online, there is now less need to lump products and consumers into one-size-fits-all containers. In an era without the constraints of physical shelf space and other bottle-necks of distribution, narrowly-targeted goods and services can be as economically attractive as mainstream fare.[3]

The more an online retailer can expose items from the long tail to consumers, the more customers with special interests and tastes it will attract. The technology that made this possible is search because it eliminates the traditional placement and advertising advantages of high-frequency products. It is search that allowed Amazon to disaggregate demand completely and ultimately to become the store for everything.

At a press conference in 2014, Bezos describes what they are trying to achieve and how it affects the consumer:

We are not trying to build a great service for tens of millions of consumers. We are trying to build a great service for one consumer. If you think about it that way, the consequences of building a great service for one consumer is you get millions.[4]

With search even the most particular preferences and needs could be matched to a niche product and a niche supplier. And when this happens, consumers really feel that the store is just built to satisfy their unique needs. As Bezos points out in the above statement, the corollary of disaggregation at scale is that it leads to extreme concentration of suppliers and consumers. Amazon attracted a large number of vendors and suppliers who sell items from the long tail and, thus, it grew beyond what any superstore or supermall could do.

But there is one more important factor in such growth stories. Disaggregation and concentration are fueled by the accumulation of data. The data about products, consumer preferences and behaviors, supplier

---

[3] Anderson, C. 2018. https://longtail.typepad.com/about.html (accessed November 12, 2019).

[4] Hunt, H. 2018. "First Mover: Jeff Bezos In His Own Words (In Their Own Words Series)." *Agate Publishing.*

prudence, and much more is what keeps the engine running and growing. The more data the company accumulates, the easier it is to answer any consumer question which, in turn, makes self-service retailing easier and frictionless.

The Socioeconomic Effects of Disaggregation at Scale

The process of disaggregation impacts not only businesses and market competition but also the operations of the job market and the market institutions. The underlying reason behind this far-reaching impact is that the technology that facilitates disaggregation is also rapidly lowering transaction costs, that is, the cost of executing a trade in the market. There is a branch of economics called transaction cost economics that studies just the effects of lowering or raising the expenses associated with the exchange of goods and services and their impact on the structure of business organizations and market institutions.

How Do Transaction Costs Affect the Job Market?

An important question in business and economic theory is why firms exist? Adam Smith argued that firms exist to facilitate the coordination of resources. The production process can be organized far more efficiently when all employees work in the same factory. The assembly line that produced the Ford Model-T makes this self-evident. Hence, the modern factory-based manufacturing system emerged and delivered big economies of scale by the use of machines and division of labor.

Ronald Coase,[5] who is considered to be one of the founders of transaction costs economics and is a recipient of the 1991 Nobel Prize in Economics, argued that firms hire employees because it is cheaper and more efficient to enter an employment contract instead of negotiating on a

---

[5] Further information on Ronald Coase's work can be found here—https://en.wikipedia.org/wiki/Ronald_Coase (accessed November 12, 2019).

daily basis the terms of the work to be done.[6] Imagine several hundred workers coming to the factory whenever they want, at whatever time they want, and deciding on the spot whether they will take on the available tasks or not. The cost of organizing work-for-hire in such a way is too high. The company would need many hiring managers to interview and explain job tasks to applicants on the spot and to coordinate the various shifts on the factory floor.

But this is exactly what Uber and other companies in the gig economy do. Uber drivers can start driving whenever they want and drive for as long as they want. They can also reject rides without having to provide any reason either to Uber or its customers. A full-time cab driver does not have the liberty to do the same.

Uber has changed the employment relationship because its device and software application make the transaction cost of contracting and paying drivers for their services very low. And while people may argue that driving does not require specialization of labor, we can see how even high-end, highly qualified services such as design, video editing, professional editing, proof reading, and many more can be organized and offered as gigs as the very successful Fiverr (fiverr.com) has done. The employment contract can be disaggregated and transformed into a freelance gig when the market demand is successfully disaggregated at scale.

But what about government and nongovernment market institutions and intermediaries?

Another Nobel Prize laurate, Douglass North,[7] argued that institutions set rules and norms that are key in determining the transaction costs in the market. Well-designed institutions lower the transaction costs and thus lead to economic growth and vice versa. Financial intermediaries exist because of their ability to lower the transaction costs. One way of doing it is by bundling together individual investor funds into a single

---

[6] In 1937 Ronald Coase published his most influential paper "The Nature of the Firm" in which he outlines the transaction cost theory about why firms exist https://onlinelibrary.wiley.com/doi/full/10.1111/j.1468-0335.1937.tb00002.x (accessed November 12, 2019).

[7] Douglass North received the Nobel Prize in 1993—https://en.wikipedia.org/wiki/Douglass_North (accessed November 12, 2019).

large fund and thus save transaction costs on the individual investors through economies of scale. As the size of the bundled fund increases, the cost of doing a larger transaction with the fund does not increase proportionally. Another example of a government intermediary is the Bureau of Motor Vehicles. One of its functions is to administer vehicle titles to ensure trust when cars are bought and sold.

But these intermediaries are expensive. What if the transaction cost can be lowered and even reduced to zero? Doesn't it imply that the intermediaries will become obsolete? If individuals can save the costs that they pay to private intermediaries to do business, they will be better off. If society does not need some of the services of government funded intermediaries, various taxes and fees can be lowered. Thirty years after the invention of the economic theory of transaction costs, a technology called blockchain promises to reduce or altogether eliminate in some cases the need for some intermediaries.

Blockchain is a universal ledger for transactional records. In the future, potentially all business transactions can be stored in this universal ledger. This is very different from the current business practice where each company has its own ledger and accounting system. In the past three decades the emergence and evolution of ERP (Enterprise Resource Planning) systems offered by Oracle, SAP, and other companies have allowed businesses to improve management and automate many processes, thus leading to significant cost savings. However, during mergers and acquisitions the integration of ERP systems is one of the costliest and most time-consuming processes. If all ERPs were built on a common universal ledger many of these due diligence and integration costs would be reduced or eliminated.[8]

Like the demand for Uber services critically depends on the reputation of the company, so the adoption and functioning of blockchain critically depends on the verification of the recorded transactions. Institutions exist in the traditional economy because verification takes time, money, and effort. How can blockchain make this verification costless?

---

[8] The first international trade financing transaction executed on blockchain shows clearly how it can lower these types of transaction costs—"HSBC Claims First Trade-Finance Deal with Blockchain" https://ft.com/content/c0670eb6-5655-11e8-bdb7-f6677d2e1ce8 (accessed November 12, 2019).

The invention of costless verification, which is built into the backbone of the blockchain technology, is the key system component that makes it possible to slash transaction costs. Blockchain stores the most important transaction attributes in individual blocks that are like virtual Lego pieces. Each subsequent modification of the transaction is recorded in a new block that is chained like a new Lego piece to the entire chain. Since the entire blockchain is replicated and distributed across many networks, it is practically impossible to corrupt the individual blocks and commit fraud.

As it can be seen, the same principle of disaggregation and scale has been applied to traditional accounting practices to make fraud quite costly and verification costless. Multiple copies of each record are stored on many random nodes of the system. If the transaction is tampered with the copies will not match. Imagine the buyer of a second-hand car who can instantly verify not only the vehicle title but also the entire prior ownership history of the car. If this can be done instantly by the buyer, the sale will occur right away, and the title transfer fee will be saved.

Blockchain Drives Creation of New Data-Driven Business Models

Since blockchain facilitates direct peer-to-peer low cost transactions, many new data-driven business models will be built directly on it. When transaction costs are low, the provision of goods and services can be disaggregated and scaled too. A new breed of decentralized software applications is emerging called dApps that allow micro peer-to-peer transactions. Using dApps people can rent the free processing power of their computers to crypto miners or other companies, can make money on their social posts as it is being now enabled by the Steemit platform, get paid for visiting locations as the Geon App allows its users to do, and many more. Like the gig economy has changed employment, dApps are changing how people can deliver and earn money on microservices because of disaggregation at scale and costless transactions. With disaggregation at scale we are seeing an economic transformation where the importance and management practices are shifting from macro- to microtrends, which in turn will change how analytics is done and now decisions are made and managed as we will discuss later in this book.

CHAPTER 6

The Two Market Competition Rules for the Digital Economy

In 2007 IBM acquired Cognos, a Canadian business intelligence software company, in an all-cash transaction for $5 billion. With this acquisition, IBM firmly established itself in the growing market for enterprise analytics. At that time, companies were starting to collect even more data and building strong analytics teams to extract insights from the data to improve all aspects of their business operations. Thus, the Cognos analytics capabilities were the perfect complement for IBM's database and integration technologies that collected, processed, and stored data. The acquisition seemed like a perfect match. Cognos offered complimentary capabilities, with strong market growth potential and opportunity to amplify sales in the other product lines too. But a perfect match does not always make a perfect fit.

A few months after the acquisition IBM approached Information Builders Inc., where I was working at the time, and started to negotiate to OEM its WebFOCUS business intelligence platform. WebFOCUS was a direct competitor to Cognos, but IBM considered it a better fit for its DB2 platform. Why OEM a competing product just a few months after a costly acquisition? Why not fix the issue?

The reason is "coopetition"—a term coined to describe a situation of cooperative competition. In 1996 Adam Bradenburger and Barry Nalebuff published a book "Co-opetition: A Revolution Mindset that Combines Competition and Cooperation" that changed the business game.

It sold more than 40,000 copies and influenced the thinking of many business executives about partnerships.[1]

The concept is not new. It is rooted in the fundamental questions of game theory about competition and cooperation. As the most popular game in game theory—the prisoner's dilemma—shows, cooperation may be desirable but is hard to attain. In the prisoner's dilemma game, two suspects are each independently offered by the prosecutor the choice to confess and betray the other and walk out free. If both suspects do not confess, they get the minimum sentence and spend a little time in prison. If both confess, they must spend a significant time in jail. Given this offer, the suspect who stays loyal to the other has the most to lose, as he will spend the maximum time in jail while the other will walk out free. If the two suspects have no means to assure each other of their silence, their rational strategy is to confess, which results in a worse sentence for both. It is one of those "damned if you do; damned if you don't" situations.

The business environment is abundant with prisoner's dilemma types of situations. You may be bidding on a contract with a partner. Suddenly the buyer reveals a much lower budget and wants both of you to cut your proposals. Who is going to take the biggest cut? What if your partner knows that you need this contract badly for your cash flow? Since you need it more than your partner, they may decline to lower their bid. Depending on how badly you need the cash, you may absorb the entire cost cut. For many years game theory scholars have studied and devised strategies of how rational people may attain and sustain cooperation in situations like this. Bradenburger and Nalebuff's book introduced the business executives to a different way of thinking about how to secure cooperation even in situations where conventional thinking would have favored direct competition.

---

[1] Here is the Amazon description of the book's impact on business: "With over 40,000 Copies Sold and Now in Its 9th Printing, Co-opetition is a Business Strategy that Goes Beyond the Old Rules of Competition and Cooperation to Combine the Advantages of Both. Co-opetition is a Pioneering, High Profit Means of Leveraging Business Relationships." https://amazon.com/dp/B004JHYREU/ref=dp-kindle-redirect?_encoding=UTF8&btkr=1 (accessed November 12, 2019).

In a big and growing market, IBM's decision to sell competing products seems completely rational. Since every competitor has enough room to expand its market share on its own, a company can maximize its profits by selling both products. Furthermore, by selling more business intelligence software, IBM can sell even more databases and more services, thus growing its other business lines too. So, did it matter to IBM that they sold competing products? No, as long as the margins were good, and the products did not cannibalize each other's growth and market share. The rationale behind coopetition is that no company or product is big enough or grows fast enough to take over the entire market.

Coopetition is neither possible nor a viable strategy in the data-driven economy. This is so because the first movers become the winners take it all companies, that is, they become the digital giants. The only two rules that govern competition in the digital economy are:

- First mover advantage, and
- The winner takes it all

These two rules are the essence of the prisoner's dilemma, except that in the new world the first suspect to confess walks out free regardless of what the second one does; that is, the first mover in the digital economy is the winner-take-it-all regardless of what its competitors do. These are the only two rules that data-driven companies use to plan their market development strategies. Traditional asset-driven companies do not understand nor take seriously these two rules as they do not fit into the aggregation, accumulation, and concentration models that are the foundation of their businesses.

First Mover Advantage

The first mover advantage concept also originated in game theory. There are special types of games in which the players move sequentially.[2] There are games in which it is advantageous to move late, as this allows you to

---

[2] For more information on sequential games visit http://kwanghui.com/mecon/value/Segment%205_5.htm (accessed November 12, 2019).

. have more information to plan your next move. The first mover advantage describes the opposite situation in which the player who moves first determines the outcome of the game.

The classical example of a first mover advantage game is "The First to 100" game. In this game two players take turns and choose numbers between 1 and 10 and add them to a cumulative total. Whoever takes the cumulative total to 100 wins the game. It is easy to see that if one player makes the cumulative total 90 or higher, the other player will win. It is also easy to see that if any of the players brings the cumulative total to 89, this will force the other player to bring the cumulative total over 90 and lose the game. We can apply backward induction to find all the numbers like 89 that will force a player on the losing path. Backward induction is another game theoretic term that describes the process of reasoning that starts from the effect and goes backwards to identify the cause. In "The First to 100" game the winning path numbers are:

100, 89, 78, 64, 56, 45, 34, 23, 12, 1

If a player wants a sure win, all they have to do is to ensure that they play first and choose the number one. After such a move the other player has zero chance to win. Naturally, experienced players never play one and then the sequence of "trap" numbers that secure the win. They play other numbers but watch carefully to be the first to claim 89. As the other player realizes the importance of 89, experienced players start securing lower "trap" numbers. All players figure out the game quickly and lose interest in it.[3]

Ironically, this is the case in the digital economy too. Once a digital giant emerges, they embark on a predictable path to capture most of the market share quickly leaving the other players without practical short-term strategies. Thus, many competitors simply disengage and fade away. Of the 20 or so search engines that were in business in the 1990s practically all faded away and today, Google has roughly 90 percent of the

---

[3] Another such game is the game of NIM, which also has winning positions. For more information on the winning strategy in NIM visit: http://gametheorystrategies.com/2012/07/05/first-mover-advantage-not-always/ (accessed November 12, 2019).

market share, Yahoo 4.2 percent, and Bing 3.5 percent.[4] Google was not the first company to invent and launch search. It had many predecessors. Google was the innovator that made search indispensable to consumers and who figured a viable monetization model on how to sell words. The first mover advantage is rarely secured by the first inventor; it goes to the innovator who drives the mass adoption with a complete business model, as Google did with its data-driven business model.

The first mover advantages exist in the physical world too. Xerox had a 15-year first mover advantage and market leadership as a result of the invention of the photocopier. Coca-Cola also had a first mover advantage secured by its highly secretive beverage recipe. In fact, patents and trade secrets exist to ensure that the first mover advantage is sustained over time being protected by a temporary legal monopoly granted by the government as a reward for ingenuity and invention of useful products.

The first mover advantage is not always sustainable in the long run. Pandora invented and launched the first digital streaming radio in 2000. The company went through its initial hurdles but started to rapidly take off in 2009. In five years, it attracted 80 million listeners[5] and became the digital radio giant. Then in 2015 it lost its leadership to a late comer Spotify. In 2018 Pandora had 100 million less active listeners than Spotify.[6] Some analysts attribute Spotify's outmaneuvering of Pandora to its curated playlists and weekly suggestions about new music for its listeners to check out.[7] Curated lists and recommendations are technology- and

---

[4] For search engine market share statistics visit https://statista.com/statistics/216573/worldwide-market-share-of-search-engines/ (accessed November 12, 2019).

[5] For detailed statistics on Pandora active listeners growth visit—https://statista.com/statistics/190989/active-users-of-music-streaming-service-pandora-since-2009/ (accessed November 12, 2019).

[6] Ingam, T. 2018. "Three Years Ago, Pandora had More Users than Spotify. Now it's Over 100m Behind." *Music Business Worldwide.* https://musicbusinessworldwide.com/three-years-ago-pandora-had-more-users-than-spotify-now-its-over-100m-behind/. (accessed November 12, 2019).

[7] Motely Fool Staff. 2017. "How Pandora Fell Behind on Streaming Music." *The Motely Fool.* https://fool.com/investing/2017/07/06/how-pandora-fell-behind-on-streaming-music.aspx (accessed November 12, 2019).

analytics-enabled strategies for disaggregation of the demand for music to meet very specific personal preferences. Spotify has created a long tail data-driven model on top of the digital streaming technology and service.

In the long term, neither a traditional assets-driven company nor a digital data-driven company is immune against market leadership take-over because of its initial first mover advantage. Myspace, the first and hugely popular social network, was overtaken by Facebook. Ford domi-nated the market with its Model T initially but by 1927 GM surpassed it in sales and market share. Can Tesla maintain its first mover advantage in the electric car market segment—this is yet to be seen. Whether a company can maintain leadership depends on many factors, but a head start is an undisputed advantage especially in the digital economy where assets-based barriers to entry for rapid scale do not exist.

In the physical assets-driven economy, the first mover advantage derives primarily from two sources: (1) market learning and (2) econ-omies of scale. Innovation, know-how, marketing strategies, customer knowledge, and so on, all pertain to market learning, while economies of scale are realized through investments in business assets. In the digital economy the first mover advantage is associated with network effects and the formation of consumer habits. The more people who join Facebook or LinkedIn the less incentive people have to join other competing social networks, as one can find pretty much everyone in one of those social or professional networks. Because one can find everything on Amazon, everyone buys and sells on Amazon. At some point the network effect transforms into a personal habit and habits hardwire the loyalty of con-sumers to digital businesses.

Hardwired habits make it very difficult for consumers to switch from their preferred digital products. Look at how hard it is for iOS users to switch to Android. It is not the physical phone that consumers become so used to as all smartphones are very much the same today. It is the interac-tion with the software, the habits that people formed about how to recog-nize and find things on the screen. Even though the same apps with the same look and feel and functionality exist on both operating systems, it is the little differences that irritate people and cause them to hate switching phones. On the other hand, people switch cars, hotel rooms, and other purely physical goods easily. Consumers do not care what brand the rental car is. They will gladly take the cheapest model in their preferred category. But try to swap their phones or tablets! Hardwired habits to digital products last long.

Because of the network effects and the emotional attachment to digital products, the winners can not only take it all but can also sustain their leadership and market dominance for very long periods of time.

The Winner Takes It All

The ABBA hit song "The Winner Takes It All" has the following lyrics:

> I've played all my cards
> And that's what you've done too
> Nothing more to say
> No more ace to play
> The winner takes it all
> The loser standing small.[8]

ABBA's song is about a relationship breakup, but it sums it brilliantly that when the winner takes it all the loser is left without any options and with diminished importance.

Mark Andreesen described the emergence of the winner takes it all effect in the digital economy in 2013:

> In normal markets, you can have Pepsi and Coke. In technology markets, in the long run, you tend to only have one …The big companies, though, in technology tend to have 90 percent of the market share. So, we think that generally these are winner-take-all markets. Generally, number one is going to get 90 percent of the profits. Number two is going to get like 10 percent of the profits, and number three through ten are going to get nothing.[9]

---

[8] Abba. 1980. "The Winner Takes It All." Track 2 on *Super Trouper*, Polar, 1980. https://genius.com/Abba-the-winner-takes-it-all-lyrics

[9] Quote   source—https://fs.blog/2018/09/mental-model-winner-take-all/. (accessed November 12, 2019).

The winner-take-all describes a market where the winner captures a large percentage of the market share. But what is surprising is how extreme the level of market share that the winner-takes-all captures in the digital economy. The traditional hospitality market used to be dominated by a few big hotel chains—Hilton, Marriott, Radisson, NH Hotels, and many more. Many other hotel chains were national—operating just within the boundaries of one country or region. Airbnb has become the dominant player in the short-term rental market and there is no other digital short-term rental company that has a market share even close to Airbnb's market share. There are also no notable regional, country-specific competitors or challengers to Airbnb's model and dominance.

This extreme market share and demand concentration is explained by Taleb in his book "The Black Swan":

> The web produces acute concentration. A large number of users visit just a few sites such as Google, which at the time of this writing has a total dominance. At no time in history has a company grown so dominant so quickly—Google can service people from Nicaragua to Southwestern Mongolia to the American West Coast without having to worry about phone operators, shipping, delivery, and manufacturing![10]

And so do Airbnb and Uber. There are no constraints to their growth because there are no physical resources involved in their business models.

In the digital economy the winner-take-all correlates with staying power. The larger the market share, the harder for anyone to challenge the digital giant. Microsoft Bing, Ask, and other search engines have been trying to challenge Google's dominance and chip away market share unsuccessfully for many years. In the traditional economy GM overtook the dominating Ford with its Model T in just a few years, and Pepsi split the market with Coca-Cola. But why is it so difficult then to challenge the winners in the digital economy?

---

[10] Quote source https://fs.blog/2018/09/mental-model-winner-take-all/ (accessed November 12, 2019).

As the accumulation of physical assets provided market protection to companies in the traditional economy, so does the accumulation of data in the digital economy. The more data and data processing power a company has, the more it can disaggregate services and products and offer a more personalized experience to win and retain satisfied customers. The more people enjoy the personalized experience, the more likely they are to form a hardwired habit and a large network. Convenience leads to habit formation and once habits are formed behaviors become automatic. Once behaviors become automatic, it is very hard for a competitor to even convince a user to try an alternative product. Only a very differentiated competitor offering even more personalized service can penetrate the stronghold of the incumbent market leader. Spotify grabbed the leadership position from Pandora because it offered a habit-forming convenience to explore and learn new music. Pandora on the other hand offered a great and easily accessible service, but there was not a habit-forming hook besides the ability to start and choose a radio station with a few taps on your phone. In the world of data and data products one can only compete with better data and better analytics directly embedded in the products and the business models.

Disrupting and Winning With Data

In today's business environment data creates the foundation for scale and scope expansion without the limitations of assets accumulation. Because of this it can disrupt any business and any market as it takes an important component of the business equation valid for the traditional asset-driven economy. The basic accounting formula that has been used since the 14th century stipulates that the company assets must equal the company liabilities plus the owners' equity. But what happens when assets are taken out of the equation? We do not know yet how to factor the value of data as an asset into this equation, but we know that data creates tremendous shareholder value and market power with less investment in physical assets.

Data is beginning to permeate every business and every physical product. Data flows in phones, watches, cars, and industrial and medical equipment, thus is becoming the most essential component that defines the usefulness of all products. But more importantly, it contains the individual DNA of the operations of each individually used product. Data makes every smart watch unique. It is not any more this or that brand, it is the watch of this individual because the data reveals how it is used, how it benefits its owner, and how it can be improved to deliver even more value.

The rest of this book will describe how data can be used to create different data-driven business models. Each model provides a conceptual framework to help companies ideate and create their own transition strategies to the digital economy and infuse their products and services with data.

PART II

Data-Driven Business Models

Information Technology is at the core of how you do your business and how your business model itself evolves.
—Satya Nadella, CEO of Microsoft Inc.

The reason why it is so difficult for existing firms to capitalize on disruptive innovations is that their processes and their business model that make them good at the existing business actually make them bad at competing for the disruption.
—Clayton M. Christensen, Kim B. Clark Professor Of Business Administration at The Harvard Business School of Harvard University.

CHAPTER 7

Asset-Less Business Models

"The four largest companies today by market value do not need any net tangible assets. They are not like AT&T, GM, or Exxon Mobil, requiring lots of capital to produce earnings. We have become an asset-light economy."[1]—Buffet told 40,000 shareholders in 2018. The four companies he referred to are Amazon, Apple, Alphabet, and Facebook and they represent about seven percent of the total market value.

However, the asset-less business model was popularized not by these four companies. It is Uber and Airbnb that made asset-less the symbol of the new economy. The two companies dominate the business news because their business models and practices challenge all traditional business assumptions and the entire regulatory foundation. How did an asset turn into a liability when it comes to business growth? Traditionally banks have financed companies' growth by securing loans with assets. But many asset-less companies have raised millions of dollars without having anything to offer as a security. Gigs versus employment? Licensed cabs versus freelancers? International sales and profits taxation on companies that have substantial sales without local operations? These and many more questions have turned the asset-less business model into a public debate about the future organization and regulation of business.

Unlike the big four, Uber and Airbnb dismantled the very foundation of the traditional business models—asset ownership and employment, in a way that made it obvious to everyone—the businessman, the employee, the regulator, and society at large. They showed that business as usual could be transformed in an unexpected way and that while society was ready to take on the transformation immediately, the legal and regulatory

---

[1] Seessel, A. 2018. "Warren Buffet Used to Avoid Tech Stock. Now he Loves Them." http://money.com/money/5484552/value-investing-embraces-tech/ *Money* (accessed November 12, 2019).

environments were not quite there to support the transformation. The questions and debates fueled the news and served both companies quite well as it is free advertising. Reading so much about Uber and Airbnb makes anyone willing to try them.

Some people call this model the "sharing economy" as people who rent their private apartments on Airbnb "share" their personal property and lifestyle with others. They let strangers into their homes. But as some analysts have pointed out, "sharing" shows the social effect while ignoring the economic effect.[2]

JP Morgan Chase categorizes the economic effects of Uber and Airbnb in the following way. Uber is a labor platform that mobilizes people to perform a task or a service and Airbnb is a capital platform where people trade assets utilization.[3] Yet, in both cases the participants bring the assets and do the services. The Uber driver brings his car into the platform and performs the service. The Airbnb apartment owner maintains the property. Prior to Uber and Airbnb, the companies providing short-term rentals had to own and maintain the assets that they rented.

In the asset-less models the excess capacity that individuals own is being put into a previously unintended use in order to produce income. The person who bought a car for personal use did not purchase it with the intent to drive for Uber. Uber just created an opportunity that previously did not exist, which changed the mindset of many car owners. Buying an apartment to live in is rarely done with the intent to use it also as a short-term rental. People typically buy either a personal or an investment property, but Airbnb blurred this line. The economic driver for the changing mindset is the extra income. Everyone needs a little extra money, and if it is easy to earn, why not do it?

This economic windfall is changing the social and individual preferences for property ownership and usage. More and more people are

[2] Smith, A. 2016. "How Americans Define the Sharing Economy." *Pew Research Center.* https://pewresearch.org/fact-tank/2016/05/20/how-americans-define-the-sharing-economy/ (accessed November 12, 2019).

[3] Farrel, D. 2016. "The Online Platform Economy." *JP Morgan Chase Institute.* PDF File. https://jpmorganchase.com/corporate/institute/document/jpmc-institute-online-platform-econ-brief.pdf

starting to think of dual usage of every asset that they buy. As statesidein-vestor.com projects: "It's 2050, and we don't think of our spaces as office buildings, retail buildings, residential or hospitality buildings anymore. It's all about maximum utilization, and you can rent space for work, living, or vacationing. It's all lumped in."[4]

Such preference for maximum utilization impacts what people purchase and how the purchased assets are financed. The extra cost of a larger apartment or a better car that can be put into a dual usage plan can be financed through the extra income from their part-time commercial utilization in the gig economy. Hence, the impact of the asset-less business models is not limited just to the way businesses operate and to how employment is structured. The effects have spread to how personal property-related decisions are being made. These personal decisions will impact how banks lend money, how properties are managed and maintained, how apartments and houses are designed and furnished, and many more. When the lines between personal and business use are blurred, many asset-related decisions change and the changes create unforeseen new business opportunities and new emerging business ecosystems.

The digital giants who have mastered the asset-less business model know how to create easy-to-earn extra income opportunities that draw in people and drive their phenomenal growth.

Indicators for Scale and Scope Potential

Success in the start-up world lures more investment both into competitors and into innovative alternations of the core business model. Investors believe that if there is one unicorn, there will be another, and even a small unicorn is a good investment. Alternative use cases are even more appealing as replication is faster than invention. Hence, we see over and over new start-ups that vary the goods, services, and other parameters of a successful new business model. Some succeed but many fail, as new

---

[4] "The State of Short Term Rentals, Its Challenges and the Opportunities Ahead." September 2018 https://housingwire.com/articles/46393-in-the-pipeline-short-term-rentals-are-the-future-of-commercial-real-estate/

business models are like cooking recipes. Changing one ingredient can spoil the meal.

What are the core factors that determine the scale and scope potential of an asset-less business model? This question is particularly relevant in the digital economy where the first mover advantage and the winner-takes-it-all effect limit the potential of new entrants as we have discussed earlier.

There are four key factors that determine the scale and scope of an asset-less data-driven model and every entrepreneur or company contemplating to launch or diversify by deploying an asset-less business model should consider and address the challenges and advantages as they relate to each factor:

- *Type of Asset*: What is the type of asset that can be offered in an asset-less business model? As we discussed earlier, the choice of selling books versus selling wine online might have made all the difference why Amazon succeeded.
- *Asset Density*: Are there enough assets to be shared within the chosen markets? Do you have enough rooms or apartments to rent in any given city to make it worth for prospects to even look up availability on your website?
- *Earning Potential*: Are there enough suppliers willing to share their assets to earn the extra income? Is the extra income sufficient and easy to earn in order for suppliers to jump onboard of an asset-less monetization platform?
- *Ecosystem Pull*: Would an ecosystem form around the platform and pull additional participants who may offer complimentary services? In some countries, car owners rent their cars to Uber drivers. In other countries, property managers take over the Airbnb management on behalf of the owners for a small fee.

These factors can be mapped to two dimensions that determine the business potential. "Easy to Monetize" is the supplier dimension, because the less effort it takes to rent out an asset or to put it into an alternative use, the more likely it is that many people will do it. "Easy to Get" is the demand dimension because the easier it is to book a room on Airbnb, the more likely it is many people choose to do it. Within this framework it can be illustrated how the types of asset, density of assets, supplier incentives, and ecosystem impact the scale and scope potential of the asset-less business.

Figure 7.1 shows why some asset-less short-term rental model businesses are more scalable and expandable than others.

The benchmark for success is Airbnb and Uber. But adopting the Uber success model to other types of assets did not always work. Two companies (AUTOnCAB and HAY BOB) failed to succeed as Ubers for rickshaws. Even though they launched in cities where rickshaws were widely available and used routinely, the businesses failed because they did not make it any easier for the rickshaw operators to monetize their assets. Rickshaws were easy to get to begin with, so the model failed because it was not easy to monetize. A rickshaw hailing app did not provide any more easy income earning opportunities to the rickshaw drivers or riders.

Similarly, companies like BlackJet that tried to sell or rent seats on private jets failed because they did not address the "Easy to Get" dimension. While it is easy for airplane owners to offer their excess capacity,

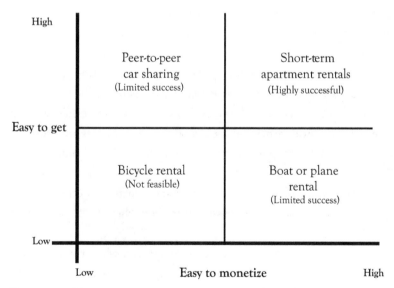

Figure 7.1 Monetization opportunity matrix: *Asset-less business model*

the scheduling of a flight is extremely complicated. A commercial jet has a fixed schedule. An Uber in Manhattan is a few minutes away from the passenger. But a private jet has neither a fixed schedule nor can be hailed at a moment's notice. The jet's location can change before the schedule and make it very uneconomical to pick up the passenger from another airport.

Short-term peer-to-peer car rentals pose many small inconveniences that make the model hard to operationalize. Most commercial car rental companies have convenient locations for travelers to pick and drop cars. But private cars stay at peoples' homes. The chances of having a sufficient supply of cars near an airport and having convenient transportation to the pickup location are very slim. Hence, it is quite difficult and inconvenient for customers to use the service. Given the inconvenience, consumers consider the alternatives—renting a car or riding Uber. These are often easier substitutes that impede the success of the peer-to-peer car rental model and limit its scope.

Finally, bikes and scooters are extremely difficult to share as there are far more inconveniences in sharing small equipment than big equipment like the personal cars. Thus, most bikes and city scooters short-term renting companies own and maintain the assets. There are over 50 start-ups in this category that use the data and analytics to optimize the utilization of their own assets, and none that does peer-to-peer sharing.

Mapping a business proposal to the Monetization Opportunity Matrix is not meant to discourage companies from starting an asset-less business. Just the opposite, it shows clearly the good and the bad in the way of making a successful business. These obstacles and challenges that can make or break a new business model are simply opportunities for innovation. Like Zappos invented a way to assure its customers that it is regret-free to buy shoes online, so some companies will invent ways to make asset-less work for personal cars, planes, boats, and other types of properties. Creativity and innovation work best when the constraints are clearly understood.

Spacious (spacious.com) is a case in point. Just when you think that it is hard to find a new short-term rental opportunity, Spacious figured out how to transform restaurants into co-working spaces. There are plenty of empty restaurants during the day that offer better and more diverse ambience than the established co-working spaces. People like to work in cafes, so why not restaurants if they are accessible. For the restaurant, the extra income is not limited just to rent. Coffee beverages and snacks can be served too. And if you work there, why not schedule the business lunch there too? Mapping the model to the opportunity matrix reveals a high potential. The asset type is good, the density of restaurants is high, the earning potential for restaurant owners is attractive, and an ecosystem can evolve.

Why Is the Asset-Less Model So Advantageous?

The asset-less data-driven business model offers three district advantages that explain the rapid growth of the companies that successfully plan and execute it.

First, it bypasses the accumulation of physical assets. If there are enough people willing to exchange their excess capacity for money, your company will get very big very quickly. Whether you are growing a fleet of cars or rentals across the world, the path to market dominance is very fast. It is contingent only on good marketing and flawless execution. But in the presence of a large number of underutilized assets, even marketing is easy because who does not want to earn extra money.

Second, the model eliminates the maintenance and support of these assets. The offered assets come with support and maintenance built-in, as their owners are directly responsible for it. The condition of the asset reflects on the owner's reputation, which ultimately determines the owner's earnings potential within the system. The transfer of the support and maintenance responsibilities to the owner makes the organization not only asset-less but also organizationally light, as it eliminates many functional departments, divisions, and corporate hierarchies that often slow and make less efficient the entire process.

Finally, the pricing of the excess capacity is very different compared with traditional markets. Pricing in the asset-less model is both market-driven, based on the willingness of consumers to pay, and owner-driven, based on the owner's needs and preferences. The owner's desire to earn extra income is frequently not based on return on investment calculations or targeted profit margins, as the asset is not purchased for business or as an investment. Thus, for many gigsters the incremental income is just that—extra money, and the price is determined by how badly the owner needs or wants the extra money. In the gig economy, supply is not always constrained by cost factors. An Uber driver can accept a low fare just because the ride is on the way back to his home. A renter may accept a low rent because she is going on vacation and needs the extra cash. A restaurant has already covered its cost, so it can rent the space as co-working at a lower rate.

Why Consumers Like the Sharing Business Models?

Contrary to common business sense, it is not just the price that matters. In many cases it is the variety. Big hotel chains and big limo service companies heavily promote the consistency of their services. All limos are big black cars. All Marriott rooms have the same look and feel. This is the traditional concept of branding. The consumer must recognize the brand right away.

But humans like diversity and novelty. Psychologists have conducted many experiments and determined that slight variations do not excite the brain as much as complete novelty.[5] The brain rewards us for the detection of novelty by releasing more dopamine—the "reward" chemical that makes us feel good and excited. But the traditional branding theory relies on variation and not on complete novelty. The rooms may look different, but small ques and patterns make us recognize instantly that this is the Marriott or the Hilton. But Airbnb property renters have neither branding standards nor corporate decorators, artists, and marketers. Each property reflects the unique taste and aesthetics of its owners.

Humans like to peek into the lives of other people and the shared economy gives people a chance to do exactly this. In a world where people have less time to socialize, the shared economy provides an outlet for this innate human need. When you rent a personal apartment, you see how people live. You feel more part of the city that you are visiting when

---

[5] Cooper, B.B. 2013. "Novelty and the Brain: Why New Things Make Us Feel So Good". *Life Hacker.* https://lifehacker.com/novelty-and-the-brain-why-new-things-make-us-feel-so-g-508983802 (accessed November 12, 2019).

you stay in a local house. You are a "guest." You learn from the décor, the appliances, the utensils, and the neighbors how people live. Sometimes the experiences can disappoint us; other times they delight us. Yet, this makes it even more authentic as it happens in our own homes too. And it also happens in hotel chains.

The fundamental need for more unique and authentic experiences is what is on the mind of every marketer today. How do we create a segment of one and tailor products and services just for that individual? The asset-less companies seem to have stumbled by accident into what consumers crave. Consistency versus variety is the new marketing battlefield. The two approaches are represented in the two different business models which today coexist. But judging by growth and market valuations of the asset-less companies, it appears that they are taking the lead driven not just by cheaper prices but also by the innate human needs for novelty and authenticity.

CHAPTER 8

Data Products as a Business

Business models based on data products are even better than the asset-less business models because they do not have to mobilize asset suppliers and service providers. Data products are sold like physical products but do not incur the cost of manufacturing, supply chain management, services and repair, and more to the same extent as physical products do. Thus, the organizational model becomes even lighter as no divisions are needed to manage these functions. Indeed, two of the big five asset-light companies that Buffet mentioned in his 2018 speech to shareholders—Google and Facebook—sell pure data products.[1]

As with other digital transformations, the transition to data products was not instantaneous. Many of the earlier products were offered for free to lure customers, and many companies like Google and Facebook had to create new ways to monetize data. A freemium model is unthinkable in the physical world because of the manufacturing costs. But even this is changing when data can make the utilization more valuable than the ownership of the asset, as we will discuss in the chapter on Products-as-a-Service business model.

Today, data products take a big share of our daily attention. Smartphone users spend 3 hours and 10 minutes per day on the phone of which 90 percent is spent in apps.[2] What if we add the extra time spent on data products on desktops, tablets, smart watches, and other devices? The statistics are clear that today people spend more time interacting with

---

[1] Google has made a move to sell physical products such as Nest and Google Home Assistant. These are data driven products that give Google more opportunities for data monetization.

[2] Wurmser, Y. 2019. "Time Spent with Media 2019." *eMarketer.* https://emarketer.com/content/us-time-spent-with-mobile-2019 (accessed November 12, 2019).

data products than with physical products. My car dashboard tells me that I spend an hour and half per day in the car. But even then, my driving experience is infused with digital experiences. I look at the GPS, listen to streaming radio or audio books, and do things that drivers should not do—check Facebook, Instagram, or LinkedIn. The navigation system further engages me by delivering information that I do not want to ignore—traffic conditions, roadside attractions, and much more. Many drivers admit that they look more often at the car computer screen than at the rearview mirror. We also check the data apps while we bike and run to get feedback on our performance despite the dangers of swerving or stumbling.

In 2014 Forbes magazine defined three types of data products that were on the raise: (1) benchmarking data products used to compare performance, (2) recommendation engines that assist people in making choices, and (3) predictive data products that help users form expectations about the future.[3] However, today those are more likely to be found as features of data products. A simple data product is the weather app. It repackages weather data from hard to access data sources and makes it conveniently available to consumers. It is so useful that people check it nearly as often as they check the time. And it provides you with weather comparisons between locations and weather predictions.

Data products are not only here to stay; they are winning over by replacing or augmenting the physical products, thus gaining more users and more usage. The online encyclopedias have made the print editions extinct. Location and mapping apps have won over paper maps, but the cute pop-up city maps invented by Stephen Van Dam are still hanging in as many tourists love them. The endurance of this palm-size origami paper map is largely due to its aesthetic appeal and perception as a novel artform. When these enduring physical products are in coopetition with similar data products, their utility is often augmented by the data products. If information is missing on the pop-up map, it can easily be

[3] Lutz Finger. 2014. "3 Data Products You Need To Know." *Forbes*.https://forbes.com/sites/lutzfinger/2014/08/19/3-data-products-you-need-to-know/#7354fba66f60 (accessed November 12, 2019).

obtained from Google, Yelp, or other apps that offer very relevant and up-to-date information.

All physical products are constrained by size, shape, weight, and time. Data products have the competitive advantage of being infinitely extensible without constraints. The origami map may fit in your back pocket, but the unfolding can never pack as much information as a data product can deliver. Printed information can only be relevant as of the day of the printing. But data products are like "breaking news," offering the most up-to-date information. Checking Yelp can show you the hot restaurant that just opened. Whether we are talking about search apps, review apps, chat apps, or social media apps, they all make us feel in-the-know.

These examples point to the existential dynamics between the physical and digital products. As the transition from physical to digital unfolds, the product markets are full of competition, coopetition, creative destruction, and previously unseen innovations. Some physical products will become obsolete and others will be augmented with complementary experiences. New products are emerging to satisfy needs and wants for which no physical products ever existed. There are also physical products that theoretically can be replaced by digital products, but it is not practical or economical to do so. Many products can only be offered as physical products, but even they are being transformed through digital fusions that we will discuss separately later in this book.

By understanding the competitive dynamics between the physical and data products, companies can make better decisions about product launches and product life cycle management. Timing the transition to digital products too early may not attract customers; while timing it too late may result in sunk costs. The failure of Encyclical Britannica management to see the obsolescence of its print edition in the raise of online competitors has been made the premier case study for late change management. Why did they need a catastrophic event—the plummeting of sales from 120,000 to 30,000, to consider and accept the necessity for change?[4] Missing on opportunities like we discussed earlier in this book is the side effect of past success. Emotional attachment and hardwired belief

---

[4] Cauz, J. March 2013. "Encyclopedia Britannica's President on Killing Off a 244-Year-Old Product." *Harvard Business Review* 9, no. 1, pp. 39–42.

that habits do not die easily is why managers resist to acknowledge the apparent obsolescence of long-term successful physical products.

Product Adoption and Replacement Dynamics

There is a strong relationship between habits, needs, and convenience that allows us to better assess the competitive dynamics between physical and digital products. The Competitive Dynamics Matrix below illustrates the relationship between habits and convenience in satisfying a need with a product. The matrix can be used to determine the timing, longevity, and coexistence of physical and digital products.

The "Habit Stability" dimension shows the relationship and transition from stable and well-established habits to newly forming habits. Habits make behaviors automatic. Once we learn how to ride a bicycle, we stop thinking how to keep balance. Automatic habits keep people entrenched in their behaviors and product preferences. New habits are formed either because new needs arise or because existing needs can be satisfied in a new and more beneficial way. Replacing old habits with new habits is not

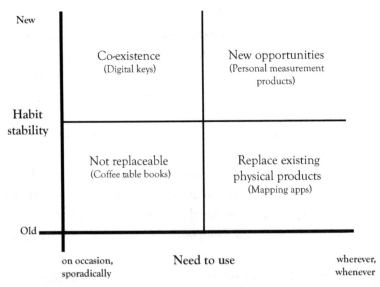

Figure 8.1 Competitive dynamics matrix: **Data products**

effortless. Psychologists call this process "the habit replacement loop."[5] To learn how to use Google maps versus a paper map requires attention, focus, and purposeful repetition. People are easily convinced to try new ways of doing things. But they also become easily frustrated when their automatic actions do not yield immediate results. People subconsciously benchmark how quickly they get things done the old way versus the new way, and feel intimidated when things they used to do without much thinking become suddenly extra hard. Their pride of having mastered a task suffers when learning a new habit.

The second dimension—"Need to Use," is the force for change in life. The more convenient it is to use a product, the more incentives people have to change their old habits. Data products have a distinct advantage in this aspect as they are portable. They fit on a phone, tablet, and laptop. They can be accessed from one's own device or from any connected device. The physical products take space and have weight. Miniaturization, the process of making physical products smaller and less bulky, evolved precisely to alleviate this pain. While we can carry only a limited number of physical products, we can load or access unlimited number of data apps on an origami-size smartphone. The convenience of portability has created an insatiable demand for data products. Wherever we are and whenever we need information, we can get it through a data product that is or can be downloaded on the phone (Figure 8.1).

Based on the Competitive Dynamix Matrix we can see that it is easiest to launch a new product that requires the formation of new habits when there is not an existing physical product. Personal measurement apps such as the apps that track sports activities or health care status are just two examples. Strava (strava.com) allows people to record their sports activities and track or benchmark their training and progress. People who train know how important such data is. But aside from stop watches there were no physical products to do this easily. With Strava and other similar apps one can track the activity with unprecedented detail—speed, distance, route map and segments, elevation, heart rate, and much more.

---

[5] Luskin, B.J., Ed.D., LMFT. 2017. "The Habit Replacement Loop." *Psychology Today*. https://psychologytoday.com/us/blog/the-media-psychology-effect/201705/the-habit-replacement-loop (accessed November 12, 2019).

The benefits are obvious and desirable and thus drive instant adoption. The learning experience is not obstructed by the habit replacement loop.

It is also easy to see why location information apps are easy to adopt. The ability to locate and find a route to a destination wherever you are and whenever you need it gradually wins over even the most habitual individuals. It often happens through the force of necessity, as sooner or later every person finds himself in a situation where he needs directions but does not have a physical map in his briefcase. Once Google rescues you from such a situation, you become a convert to the new way of doing things. Because life exposes us to many such AHA moments, the data products keep finding new user segments. My sister was a staunch opponent to using Facebook until she went on a charitable mission in Kenya. When she left, she wanted to stay in touch and share stories and pictures with the local community. The convenience of Facebook was undeniable and now we all suffer picture overload from this new staunch Facebook user. Even though she still prints pictures and shows them to people, her old habit coexists with the new habit.

There are many digital products that call for the formation of new habits but do not replace or make obsolete the old habits. Applications like Kisi create digital keys that unlock the doors in office buildings. There are many variations of Kisi. Some hotels deliver your room in their branded mobile apps. Thus, you do not have to see the concierge. These apps are replacing the plastic key cards and the traditional metal keys. But the adoption is slow, and the old habits coexists with the new habits in clearly delineated use cases. While many people use digital keys to get in the office building and to their office floor, many still prefer metal keys for their personal offices. While some people use the hotels' apps to open their rooms, others like to stop by and get their key card from the concierge along with recommendations for nearby restaurants and other amenities. And not many people are replacing their home keys with digital keys. This is driven by the Need-to-Use as there is no compelling reason to make a universal switch to digital keys.

Finally, there are physical products that can be replaced but it is not economical or practical to do so. Such products are typically used only on occasion and in very specific settings like the coffee table books and magazines that we see in waiting rooms and hotel lobbies. Even though people can find the same information online, they prefer to browse the physical books and magazines. The activity is not purposeful. The person just happened to be there, and something grabbed their attention—the cover image, the title, or just the colorful combination on the front cover. If they wanted to discover or find some particular information, they will do so on their phone using a data app. Coffee table books are part of the décor and are intended to distract us from thinking about time by arousing our curiosity. Neither the iPhone nor a tablet placed on the table can do that as they do not have a cover page. Devices can only alert us that something known to us or something that we are looking for is occurring. Hence, coffee table books seem indestructible at least for the moment.

There are many digital product failures because people try to replace old habits or create new habits without taking into account the nature of the habit and its relationship to the need to use a product. Some data product architects think that information is the sole driver to habit formation. But an app that tells you how many eggs are left in your refrigerator like the Quirky Egg Minder is not worth even downloading. Every time you take an egg, you see how many are left. And in the supermarket, you need a consolidated shopping list instead of a bunch of apps tracking separately each item in your refrigerator. The design starts with the understanding that the habit and the need that you want to reshape with a new data app is the entire shopping list. This may be doable or not because the idea that every habit can be digitized is false.

Indicators for Scale and Scope Potential

The Competitive Dynamics Matrix tells us how a data product will fit and exist in the physical world. The economic performance of the data product can be assessed by looking at the Monetization Opportunity Matrix. What are the key factors that affect the scale and scope potential of a new data product?

The monetization opportunity can be mapped to two dimensions that reflect the breadth and depth of the data product usage which ultimately determines its scale and scope. The "Specificity" dimension indicates whether a product is designed for a very broad or very narrow purpose and use cases. The "Frequency of Use" dimension defines the

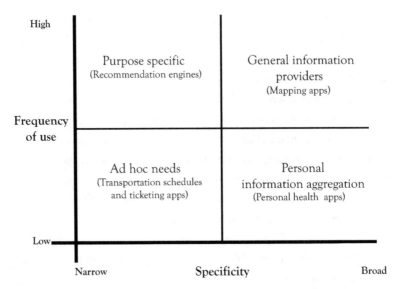

Figure 8.2 **Monetization opportunity matrix: *Data products***

intensity of the habit. The four key factors from the asset-less business model are slightly modified to reflect the pure digital nature of the data products. The type of asset is replaced by the specificity of the product and the density of assets is replaced by the frequency of use. In other words, the physical and location characteristics of the assets in the asset-less business model are replaced with the digital characteristics of the data products. Even though the monetization opportunity is conceptually the same, the physical and digital products have fundamental differences that are reflected in the Monetization Opportunity Matrix in Figure 8.2:

Maps are typically narrowly defined. They depict a geographic area and some meaningful information about the area such as roads, buildings, and so on. But location information is a very broad category as maps can be overplayed with layers of useful information such as population statistics, historical information, commercial information, and much more. Hence, a location information product, such as Google maps, can have a very broad usage. Products like that can be overlaid with more and more information, but they reach a saturation point where more becomes overload. Hence, the broad location information apps will always coexist with location information products with narrow specificity. Data apps that provide information on parking locations such as Boxcar (http://boxcarapp.com) coexist in a co-opetition with Google maps. Data products with a broad specificity and high frequency of usage offer multiple monetization opportunities. Each layer of information can be monetized separately. They also drive the creation of large ecosystems because applications with narrow specificity can be built on top of them. A parking finder app can leverage Google maps.

Personal health apps have a broad use as people can connect multiple devices to track various vitals but low frequency of use. General purpose, less frequently used apps are harder to monetize, and thus the opportunity is limited to what the end users are willing to pay or to how much the device manufacturers are willing to subsidize the end users. Very often the device manufacturers own the apps. While this may work for large device manufacturers with many devices, smaller ones end up facing the problem of narrow specificity and low usage frequency. Users do not want to install and manage information in separate very specific but rarely used apps. The monetization opportunities increase significantly when such apps are used for continuous 24/7 monitoring. For people with chronic conditions continuous monitoring makes the app the most used and useful of all apps. Continuous monitoring can be appealing to healthy people, too, who want to control risks during exercise or on-the-job stressful activities.

We all are amazed by Amazon and Netflix's ability to recommend products and movies that are very relevant to us. LinkedIn recommends new connections. There are many search and recommendation engines that work extremely well for very specific domains—products, movies, medical research, and so on. These utilities are data products. They have been trained and continuously learn about the behaviors and preferences of individuals to aid their choices by filtering out irrelevant information. They are close-minded experts very knowledgeable about a topic, but clueless about the rest of the world. Such data products are monetized within other applications. There are "services" supporting the core business model. There are many variants of such highly specialized data products—image recognition and classification, text classifications, and so on. Many artisanal software companies develop such highly specialized data products and sell and maintain them for other companies.

The monetization opportunities for such data products are in their ability to improve and drive incremental business. If more relevant recommendations drive more purchases, companies will be willing to invest and pay more for such data products. The growth of LinkedIn from 20 million members to 400 million is frequently attributed to the "connect" recommendation pioneered by the company. The frequency of use often determines not just the monetization but also the relevancy of the recommendations as such data products learn from past experiences.

Unfortunately, such data products cannot be generalized to expand their scope and move them to the upper right quadrant. Their value derives from their accuracy, which increases by constraining the learning and recommendations to narrow domains. It is also hard to sell them to competing companies as they provide a competitive edge. People visit and spend money on sites where products are easy to find and come across. Hence, companies keep such data products proprietary and often develop them in-house. Content classification data products do not have the same problem as they are utilities that support the business but are not revenue drivers.

Narrowly defined data products with low frequency of use irritate consumers but are necessities. "Why do I have to download an app just for that ..." is the typical reaction when we have to get an app to do one thing. The NJ Transit app delivers train schedules, alerts, and digital tickets. But the schedules and alerts are not the reason why people download it. It is the digital tickets. If you want to avoid the fine for purchasing a ticket on the train, you must have the app. To overcome user frustrations, single purpose apps have to find a way to expand the breadth of useful features or merge with apps that allow the purchase of multiple types of tickets. Why not merge the NJTransit app with Amtrak or United apps? Google authenticator is also a single purpose app with low frequency of use, but because people can use it to authenticate with many sites and apps it is a must have.

Value to Consumers

Why do consumers love data products and spend so much time in apps? Data products satisfy the fundamental human needs to discover and learn new things, to seek entertainment, and to socialize. Data products have become part of all conversations as people check facts and seek information in real time during meetings and events. Apps allow us to fill or kill time with entertainment or socializing whenever and wherever we want. The less we can do this in person, the more we turn to data products and apps to fill the need. Data products have become as essential as physical products are. Many physical products are modern inventions that we learned how to use and that are now an indispensable part of our lifestyles. Apps are arguably even more indispensable. Some are useful tools that we cannot live without, whereas others provide deeper meaning as they connect and keep us connected to people.

Today and even more so in the future, many companies will rely on data products as a core source of revenues. As with physical products, managing the lifecycle of data products requires complete understanding of why, how, and what drives the adoption and the scale and scope of the data product. Because most of the data products do not start their lifecycles as obvious necessities like many physical products do, all data products have to inspire the desire to try and learn by appealing to fundamental human needs and thus drive the formation of new habits.

CHAPTER 9

Digital Supplements

Like physical products, digital products can have many variations. But the economics of versioning is very different. In the digital world, versioning is a revenue multiplier, while in the physical world it is a pricing instrument. Thus, digital versions are not created to just lower the prices by offering cheaper substitutes. Paperback editions are a cheaper substitute for hardcover books. This kind of versioning is a price instrument because by lowering the price the producer gains incremental sales. Lower-priced versions segment the market by the price sensitivity of the consumers.

This strategy is well known and widely adopted in the physical world. Small and large goods have versions; brands have regular and black labels, and even software used to have home and premium editions, but this model is being abandoned and replaced by more sophisticated pricing models for digital goods.

In the digital world, versioning creates new markets and new experiences. The different versions are not exactly substitutes. In most cases they are complementary in some way. Thus, we gladly buy two or three products instead of one. On the other hand, it is hard to imagine why someone would buy the hardcover and the paperback edition of the same book. Complimentary versioning requires creativity and innovation, while the making of lower-priced substitutes requires just good accounting and lower materials and manufacturing costs.

Digital products are known to have increasing returns. Once the product is created, an infinite number of users can download or sign up to use it without any extra cost to the supplier. As product adoption grows, profits surge while costs remain more or less the same. Scaling up has only a positive upside unlike in the physical world, where diminishing returns kick-in and force producers to invest to expand production. The revenue multiplier is very different from the increasing returns. It creates new revenue streams that can be scaled to produce increasing returns.

The Kindle book and the Audible audiobook are new and completely different products even though they are made from the same ingredient—the book manuscript. The two digital versions do not have to be produced by the same company as it often happens in the physical world. Audible was founded to turn audiobooks into a mainstream product. Audiobooks existed prior to Audible, but the company really made them popular and controls according to some estimates 41 percent of the market.[1] They invented many audiobook-related technologies but most importantly Audible turned audiobooks into an artform by attracting top artists to impersonate the characters.

I started to appreciate this new artform after listening in the car to Jim Dale's recording of one of the Harry Potter books that my daughter insisted I read. How could the same voice take so many different forms so that I could recognize each character just by the changes in the tone? Our appreciation of the richness of human voice and its artistic abilities has not only made singing popular but also a big industry. Why shouldn't it be the same with reading? Because of its richness voice itself has become a source of versioning that drives more revenues. There are two recordings of the Harry Potter books by Stephen Fry and Jim Dale, and there is a heated debate about who does it better.[2] To participate in the debate, one has to buy and listen to both audiobooks.

As can be seen, the Kindle and Audible books are neither 100 percent substitutes nor 100 percent complements. I can listen to the audiobook in the car and read the Kindle on the beach. They are supplements as they offer alternative experiences that enrich, complement, and complete the overall book experience, as the different versions can be appreciated in different ways and in different settings. Such supplemental products do not cannibalize each other's sales as cheaper substitutes of physical

---

[1] Brustein, J. 2018. "Amazon Turbocharged Audible's Domination of Audiobooks." *Bloomberg Businessweek.* https://bloomberg.com/news/articles/2018-03-13/amazon-turbocharged-audible-s-domination-of-audiobooks (accessed November 12, 2019).

[2] Hall. R.S. 2013. "Stephen Fry vs. Jim Dale: The Battle of the Harry Potter Audiobooks Narrators." *Bookriot.* https://bookriot.com/2013/12/09/stephen-fry-vs-jim-dale-harry-potter-narrators/ (accessed November 12, 2019).

products do, nor fully complement each other as they cannot be consumed simultaneously as fish and white wine can be.

Digital versions can inspire new ideas, reveal synergies, and breed new products and services. They can inspire new hardware or software that make them more usable. The Kindle device has become synonymous with digital books. We shop for the Kindle editions, not for an e-book. Any digital book can be read in the PDF reader or in any browser directly. In fact, the PDF digital format was invented to make document reading easier. And yet, consumers prefer the Kindle as it enhances their reading experience and hence Amazon commands 53 percent of the market for e-readers.[3] The paper-like screen, the built-in dictionary that you can instantaneously access, the note-taking feature, the highlighting, and quotation sharing are features that make the Kindle very useful. We can take an entire library of books anywhere and store and print notes in organized ways, and also we can share passages that we like and glimpse at what other people have highlighted as interesting. Reading is a deeply social experience and we like to discuss books. The Kindle embeds the social directly in the reading experience. All of this taken together make us buy new Kindles when the hardware gets significant updates and in turn it hooks us to buying Kindle editions from Amazon.

The Kindle book is not a substitute for the print edition. Despite all fears, it has not nor will cannibalize print.[4] They are supplements. Portability is the defining supplementary feature. When you need to travel light, you take the Kindle. When you need to continue reading a book that you didn't bring with you, you can continue reading it on the Kindle app on your phone. The seamless transition from one form and device to

---

[3] MarketWatch. 2019. "eReader Market Opportunities, Market Share, Size, Regions, Revenue, Types, Applications & Forecast 2019-2025." https://marketwatch.com/press-release/ereader-market-opportunities-market-share-size-regions-revenue-types-applications-forecast-2019-2025-2019-03-27 (accessed November 12, 2019).

[4] There are many debates about the future of printed vs. digital books. This article reviews the history, the hype and the facts—"Are Paper Books Really Disappearing," By Nuwer, R. January 2016, bbc.com http://bbc.com/future/story/20160124-are-paper-books-really-disappearing (accessed November 12, 2019).

another is what makes reading anytime and anywhere very similar to how we use and benefit from the location information apps. This experience determines the ultimate scale and scope of the reading business. A reader can go from paper to device, to phone, to headphones without losing track of his book and for that convenience they are willing to pay for the multiple versions and the associated devices.

The informational symbiosis does not stop here. A core tenant of this book is that data has the magical property to create new value out of itself through subsetting, enrichment, and metamorphosis. A subset of a vast amount of environmental data is packaged in a product called the Weather app. The same weather data enriched with routes information can drive packaging optimization—the amount of ice and insulation put in the box when shipping fresh food products by companies like Plated and Blue Apron. And metamorphosis occurs when something completely new is borne from the same data. What if you wanted to create the best conversational bot? If the bot is to pass the Turing test and be able to pass as a human, it has to have a real voice and converse on many topics intelligently. It has to be able to change the intonation to express different emotions and to be able to tell stories and make arguments. We humans learn how to be good conversationalists by reading and by listening to other people. Storytelling and reading are the bedrock of our communication and reasoning abilities.

Today bots are being trained using machine learning techniques, which we will discuss in more detail in Part III of this book. The approach is similar to how humans learn. The machine is fed lots of examples to learn from. One of the hardest problems in machine learning is the collection of teaching examples. And you need a lot of examples as machine learning algorithms require a lot of training.

If you consider the digital supplements that we discussed, Amazon already has all that is needed to train a conversational bot. They have the largest collection of digital text and voice. Thus, the data scientists have the materials to train Amazon's Alexa to be intellectually and artistically sophisticated. Why this has not happened yet is a different story. There is plenty of more work to be done to make algorithmic learning as efficient as human learning is. Humans learn from just a few examples, while machines have a learning limit even with millions of examples.

Amazon's impact on the reading business is the most analyzed and widely discussed case about the enormous benefits of digital transformation. As Eric Weiner,[5] a bestselling author on innovation states, the most obvious examples are sometimes the best to make a point. The point is that data has the potential to morph continuously into new products and services. As companies collect more and more data and package it into data products, the opportunities to invent new data products increase.

The Opportunity Matrix for Digital Supplements

The dimensions in the opportunity matrix for digital supplements are modified to reflect the particulars for this type of growth model. Figure 9.1 and 9.2 shows the Monetization Opportunity Matrix for the obvious case of the reading business.

The technology dimension reflects the ability to package the new version in a new device (the Kindle) or a new app (the Audible app). Some technologies are more complex than others and the complexity

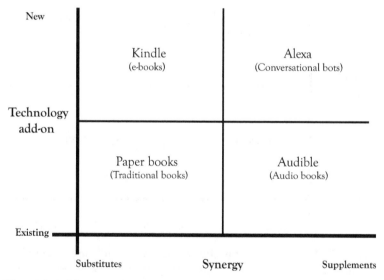

Figure 9.1 **Monetization opportunity matrix:** *Digital supplements* *(Example 1)*

[5] Weiner, E. 2016. "Geography of Genius". New York, New York: Simon & Schuster.

determines whether the technology itself will be a source of revenue, as is the case of the Kindle, or whether it will be just a distribution vehicle, as is the Audible app given for free to users. The synergy dimensions determine to what extent two versions can be used somewhat as substitutes as opposed to being complete alternatives that complement the overall experience. These have implications for the marketing of the digital versions. As we saw earlier, the Kindle sparked a lot of discussions about the future of paper books. Audiobooks on the other hand have never been considered a rival that can cannibalize print or digital books.

The ultimate synergy is a new product with an entirely new use case, as is Alexa. Alexa can deliver audiobooks or order digital and print books. But it can do a lot more. Yet, its intelligence can be enhanced by learning from the other two digital products.

Let us go to a less obvious example of digital versioning—the digitization of money.

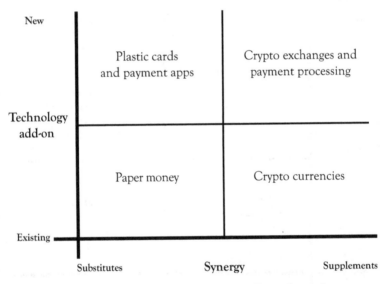

Figure 9.2 Monetization opportunity matrix: *Digital supplements* (Example 2)

Paper money is going through the same transformation process as books. Unlike the saturated market for digital books, the digitization of money is a highly competitive market with many players coming with different products to facilitate the exchange of money for goods or for money. The monetization matrix below shows the different versions of money and how synergies give birth to new types of products and services.

For centuries money has been a physical good—metal coins or paper notes. At different times commodities such as salt, tobacco, cattle, and so on, were used for payments, but coins and paper money became the standard because of their convenience. They are easy to carry and do not require special care as cattle do. Plastic cards turned out to be even more convenient especially when people travel. The notes in a stolen wallet cannot be recovered, but a plastic card can be canceled, thus minimizing the risk of actual money theft.

Plastic cards sparked the development of many related devices such as card readers for payment processing and software for transaction processing between the participating intermediaries. A complex ecosystem of hardware manufacturers, software companies, and payment processors evolved to support these digital payments. Today, the lucrative payment processing revenues have attracted many disruptive companies who are pushing the limits of digitization through payment apps that eliminate the need for a physical card. These payment apps fuel the development of new contactless hardware to easily tap the phone to make a payment. Simplicity and convenience are driving the evolution of a new ecosystem.

While plastic cards can be viewed as a substitute for paper money, crypto currencies create new money that has supplemental use cases. The crypto currencies have both advocates and critiques, but more countries and more businesses are beginning to accept them on par with paper money and plastic cards. Like the plastic cards, the crypto currencies create many opportunities for making money which attracts users and grows the ecosystem. The crypto ecosystem includes miners who unlock new coins, hardware manufacturers making specialized technologies to lower the cost of mining, and software developers who provide trading, exchanges, analytics, and fraud detection tools for the crypto operations. When money is made in the ecosystem, the digital product will grow and fuel more related innovations. The new crypto exchanges are emerging as intermediaries between paper, plastic, and crypto, but their evolution may turn them into something much bigger as they are adding fast commercial payments processing and other functions. The more digitized the ecosystem, the more services the exchanges can add and grow into new digital giants.

How to Tell If Digital Version Will Work?

Given the hype of the digital transformation, companies want to turn everything into digital. But what determines that a product—physical or digital—can be versioned successfully? First, it is necessary that the digital version meets the spec, that is, the digital product is equivalent in its core function to the original one. The digital book has the same manuscript. The digital currency can store value and can be used as a medium of exchange. But while this is enough to make a digital version usable, it is not a guarantee for success.

More often the functional equivalency is a trap for product and marketing managers. Why have two products that do the same thing? Scaling one product is hard enough, so why scale two? Even more so if the different versions require separate marketing and other resources that can impact profit margins. There is also the fear of cannibalization. When two products are just functionally equivalent, it is hard to predict whether sales will just split or increase.

Digital supplements succeed when they offer alternate experience coupled with convenience. We go to different restaurants that serve more or less the same food because the ambiance is different or because we happened to be nearby. The functional equivalency trap is false because people see value both in consistency and in variation. Consistency can bore us, and variation can tire us. Versioning retains the consistency through the functional equivalence but infuses it with variations that enrich the experience while simultaneously making it more convenient.

In blind pursuit of digitization, people fail to see the value added that makes the digital supplement viable. The Twitter Peek device launched in November 2009 was the brainchild of two very successful managers from Virgin Mobile USA. It was the Twitter equivalent of the Kindle—a dedicated handheld device just for tweeting. It met the spec 100 percent, but it failed. It did not add any value through new experiences or conveniences. The Twitter Peek belongs to the same quadrant in the Monetization Opportunity Matrix as the Kindle. If we place the smart in the quadrant below it as a base technology for this matrix, we can see that the hardware is not that new or different from what the consumers already had. Unlike the iPhone or the tablet, the Kindle has a paperwhite screen that is especially convenient for reading. The Twitter Peek also did not offer an alternative experience. What more can you do, that you cannot do on the Twitter app on the phone? There is only the inconvenience of carrying one extra device and switching between devices. The product fails the Monetization Opportunity Matrix as it cannot draw customers even as a substitute. Without extra experience and extra convenience there is no value.

Life Cycle Supplemental Add-Ons

Every physical and digital product inevitably goes through life cycle variations. Planned life cycle variations are revenue drivers and thus should be considered as part of the business model of every product. My grandfather had only two suits his entire life. They were well made and he took care of them as diligently as we take care of our cars today. Like a scheduled oil change, he took his suits to a tailor for "maintenance" every year. This was a very different behavior from our habits of buying one or two new suits every year. Being curious about this, I checked the history of men's fashion and discovered that for a very long period people purchased one or two suits for a lifetime.

And then "trends" were invented. Trends are purposefully introduced variations that induce consumers to buy more. Fashion designers vary the cut, the fit, the colors, the materials, and other features to make the old look dated. Those changes nudge people to see things differently and want new things. Some economists call this planned obsolescence and many anticonsumerism advocates are really against it. But such attacks ignore the innate human craving for novelty and the fact that novelty makes people learn new things. When novelty is driven by alternate experiences and hew conveniences the overall knowledge in society increases.

The business of life cycle variations is well developed in the world of physical goods, but it is fast invading digital product management. The life cycle variations in the digital space are different as it is less about complete change and more about continuous supplemental add-ons.

The creation of the supplemental add-ons is driven by market saturation and user learning. As more competitors enter the same space, companies start to differentiate by exploiting the user learning curve. Products get enhanced with more features that allow users to do more things. If you give users too many features too early, they will be turned off from the product because the learning curve will be too steep. If you introduce advanced features too late, users will abandon the product for being too shallow compared with other products.

The life cycle monetization matrix in figure 9.3 reflects the market and product dynamics for branding and design products, and more especially for the marketplaces that distribute such products as Shutterstock (shutterstock.com), Envato (envato.com), 123RF (123rf.com), and many more. The rapid saturation in this market drives quick product variations.

Branding and design products used to be delivered as one-off high-end services. This is why many design agencies failed to see how a brand manager could choose off-the-shelf products without consulting a creative director. The more value we place on our own services, the harder it is to foresee how technology can drive their commoditization, even though markets are designed to do that through competition and cost

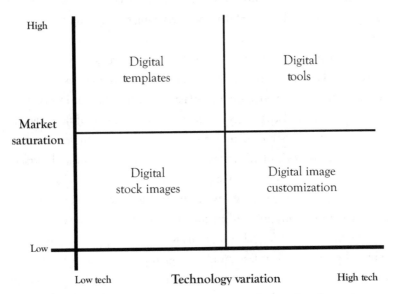

Figure 9.3 Monetization opportunity matrix: *Lifecycle adaptation*

pressures. Today even creative directors draw inspiration and source materials from these sites.

So how did a site like Shutterstock break into this market? The answer is variety—a huge variety of stock photos that no creative agency could match. That was the genius insight of Shutterstock's founder, who himself shot over 100,000 images to seed the site. Variety always finds a customer. Give people enough to look at and they will find something to buy. Both tourist gift shops and Walmart know and exploit this retail secret very well. Hence our base product for the matrix is the stock photo.

In the digital world, variety is easy to replicate. It does not take too many technologies and resources to create variety. Hence, the market for stock images became saturated very fast. The solution to this problem is to introduce supplemental add-ons. Allow users to download different sizes of the same image. This is technologically simple solution, but it allows the company to attract consumers with different needs and different price preferences. Thus, the same image can be monetized differently.

Simple templates do not require technology, but they allow consumers to customize the content. They turn the design process into a self-service where everyone, even people who do not possess artistic skills, can deliver good looking marketing content. But templates, especially those intended for web content, such as the WordPress website templates, have magical revenue potential. They turn the one-off purchase into a subscription-based recurring revenue. As browsers, web standards, and aesthetic preferences change, templates become maintainable. The company that ensures that the templates are up to date can charge subscription fees for the updates. The business value of digital is the ability to turn revenues into predictable streams via subscriptions for carefree maintenance.

The self-service model lures the customers to do more themselves. As they learn more, they want to be able to do more. This is the point at which sites add tools as means to differentiate, attract, and keep users loyal. The sites for digital marketing and branding content are introducing tools to customize layouts, build templates, and much more. Tools are another source of subscription revenue. More importantly, tools make consumers more loyal because of switching costs. Once a user has invested time and effort to learn a tool, it is difficult to persuade them to switch and learn an alternative tool. The more sophisticated the user, the harder to switch.

The life cycle supplemental add-ons allow companies to differentiate the sources of their revenues. Images are a direct sale, but templates and tools are subscription sales. Digital products can be varied and enhanced to convert one-off sales to recurring revenues.

CHAPTER 10

The Man-Less Business Model

Why did the 19th century economist David Ricardo change his mind about money and machinery?[1] Economists still speculate about the reasons. David Ricardo is one of the most influential classical economists along with Thomas Malthus, Adam Smith, and James Mill. He was a self-made millionaire who made his fortunes on financial speculations about the outcome of the battle of Waterloo. He lived in times when inventions like the steam engine and the textile mills were transforming capitalism and developed a strong interest in the effect of machines on labor. He formulated the machine/labor substitution effect, that is, the ratio at which machines can replace human labor in the production process, which is at the core of the above-mentioned speculation.

Prior to 1821 Ricardo saw the introduction of machines as beneficial. He viewed the displacement of workers by machines as a temporary inconvenience and the benefit of machine production to lower prices as a permanent gain to society. Since lower prices made many goods affordable to lower income people, machines increased the overall standards of living. Ricardo believed that the demand for labor is permanent over time and, thus, the temporarily displaced workers will eventually find new jobs. Furthermore, since machines replace low skilled jobs, workers will be retrained for higher level and higher paying jobs. Who would want to be a taxi driver today, if they can get a better paying job and ride to work in an autonomous vehicle? Ricardo's belief was based on his observations

---

[1] This scholarly article raises the question in its very title. November, 1977. "Why Did Ricardo (Not) Change His Mind? On Money and Machinery" by Shlomo Maital and Patricia Haswell, *Economica New Series* 44, no. 176, pp. 359–68.

of how machines worked at the time. He noted that: "machining cannot be worked without the assistance of men, it cannot be made without the contribution of their labor."[2]

But in 1821 he added another chapter to the revised edition of his book "The Principles of Political Economy and Taxation" in which he changed his mind:

> ... I am convinced, that the substitution of machinery for human labour, is often very injurious to the interests of the class of labourers.
>
> My mistake arose from the supposition, that whenever the net income of a society increased, its gross income would also increase; I now, however, see reason to be satisfied that the one fund, from which landlords and capitalists derive their revenue, may increase, while the other, that upon which the labouring class mainly depend, may diminish, and therefore it follows, if I am right, that the same cause which may increase the net revenue of the country, may at the same time render the population redundant, and deteriorate the condition of the labourer.[3]

Ricardo's new belief is that the substitution effect does not necessarily benefit society and that the displacement may not be just temporarily. The substitution effect is a rate. The faster the increase in the rate, the larger the profit. Today, this is known as the marginal rate of technical substitution, or the rate at which an investment in automation has to increase in order to keep the same level of production taking into account the displaced labor. Once a rate is defined, humanity will do anything to accelerate it and bring it to its logical conclusions—complete substitution.

---

[2] Ricardo, D. 2004. "The Principles of Political Economy and Taxation." Dover Publications.

[3] The original quote is in David Ricardo's third edition of his *Principles*, Chapter 31, "On Machinery," (1821). The quote here is taken from a blog post by Mark Thoma. 2012. "David Ricardo 'On Machinery'," *Economist's View*. https://economistsview.typepad.com/economistsview/2012/09/david-ricardo-on-machinery.html (accessed November 12, 2019).

Perhaps Ricardo changed his mind because he could not avoid the logical conclusions of his own argument. But, as one economist discovered, Ricardo might have changed his initial observations on how machines operate and how technology will evolve:

> In a letter to J. R. McCulloch written in June 1821, Ricardo wrote: "If machinery could do all the work that labour now does, there would be no demand for labour. Nobody would be entitled to consume anything who was not a capitalist, and who could not buy or hire a machine." (Ricardo 1951–1973 8: pp. 399–400)[4]

Ricardo foresaw that a day will come when machines will neither be operated nor be created by man. The invention of autonomous machines will lead to complete automation and to new men-less business models.

The tracking of rates typically indicates that the future is closer than we think as all effort and investment will go toward accelerating the rate. In 2016, I was invited to Lockheed Martin to brainstorm together with 90 other executives about a Condition-Based Maintenance (CBM) system for military ships. Equipment maintenance is typically done based on a predefined schedule. Every 12 or 18 months, ships are brought back to the base and many parts are serviced or replaced according to the predefined schedule. Today, most cars alert the drivers to go to the dealership for certain types of scheduled maintenance. Each type of maintenance requires the service or replacement of certain parts even if it is not needed. Once the alert goes on the dashboard, the dealership mechanic does what is required in order to turn off the alert.

But what if the ship can sail for another year without maintenance? What if you could drive another 10,000 miles? It will certainly save you money. The length of operation without defects depends on many factors and conditions, while the scheduled services and parts replacements are based on the average expected time in service without considering the variations in operating conditions. The problem with such averages is that some machines break before the scheduled maintenance and others

---

[4] Hollander, S. 2019. "Retrospectives: Ricardo on Machinery." *Journal of Economic Perspectives* 33, no. 2, pp. 229–42.

work much longer. In both cases unnecessary costs are incurred. If a ship breaks at sea, either a crew of experts has to fly to repair it or the ship has to be brought to the shore for the repair. On the other hand, if the scheduled maintenance is not really needed, the cost of early service and parts replacement is unnecessary. Condition-based maintenance is a data-driven alternative to scheduled maintenance as it delivers repairs at the point of need, that is, right before the equipment breaks. Similar to the just-in-time inventory management practice, CBM leverages data and advanced analytics to predict and deliver just-in-time services and repairs and eliminate unnecessary costs and waste.

The moderator asked us to imagine what would a military ship look like 25 years from that day. Once we had this idea, we could think backwards and design a CBM system that could be implemented with today's technologies, but also be extensible over time to meet the needs of the future ship without a complete redesign. We all agreed that the future ship would be men-less. Why put crews at sea for many months away from their families? Why risk human lives in military operations? Any rational commander would like to minimize risks and inconveniences, and best way to do that is to design a men-less ship.

One obvious suggestion was to build a remote-controlled drone ship. But a ship is a large piece of equipment sailing many miles away. Many unforeseen things can happen and interfere with the remote-controlled operations. Hence, the future ship had to have autonomy and make decisions similarly to how a crew of specialists would decide and act in certain circumstances. But what if some system on the autonomous ship breaks down while it is 10,000 miles away. Coming to shore for repairs is costly and delaying the repair exposes the ship to environmental and military risks. The future ship must be able to self-diagnose and self-heal itself. Self-diagnosis requires a robust CBM system to prevent possible equipment failures just-in-time, while technologies like 3D printing, robotic automation, and virtual reality enable autonomous or remotely assisted repair. All people in the group acknowledged the validity of the concept—a men-less, autonomous, self-diagnosing, and self-healing ship. We all thought how powerful the vision was. Why couldn't we have it sooner?

The rate of technological evolution is not a straight line. At some periods it grows exponentially and what seems a faraway future comes faster than we expect and often catches us unprepared for the social and other consequences. On April 25, 2018, the first drone ship joined the U.S. navy.[5] The ship is crewless, 140 ton, 132-foot-long autonomous sailing robot. The concept of the men-less ship was formulated in 2010 and just in six years it became a reality. It was deployed for testing in 2016 and released for service in 2018. At the time when we were discussing the distant possibilities for a men-less, autonomous ship and flattered ourselves with our thought leadership, the concept was already near its completion.

It is interesting why the army may prefer a completely crew-less ship instead of one with a few crew members who can react quickly to any emergency with the remote support of highly qualified experts. This is a general question about why we strive to develop completely autonomous machines versus hybrid technologies where humans and machines can work together to achieve the desired outcome. The rate of substation is one directional.

On July 2019, The Atlantic published an article titled "At Work, Expertise Is Falling Out of Favor."[6] It reviews an army experiment to operate a highly sophisticated multipurpose warship with significantly reduced crew. The ship could hunt submarines, sweep mines, enter combat operations, and much more. A ship of even less complexity typically required a crew of 200 highly specialized professionals, but the new ship had only 40 "hybrid" crew members. The shortage of personnel was supplemented by advanced intelligent technologies that made it possible to do more with less resources. As the author of the article pointed out the ship was a complete departure from the 240 years of management

[5] Macias, A. 2018. "The First Drone Warship Just Joined the Navy and Now Nearly Every Element of it is Classified." *CNBC* https://cnbc.com/2018/04/25/first-drone-warship-joins-us-navy-nearly-every-element-classified.html (accessed November 12, 2019).

[6] Useem, J. 2019. "At Work, Expertise Is Falling Out of Favor." *The Atlantic*, https://theatlantic.com/magazine/archive/2019/07/future-of-work-expertise-navy/590647/ (accessed November 12, 2019).

principles and operating traditions. The "hybrid" crew was essentially a band of jack-of-all-trades that replaced the traditional masters-of-one-trade. With the assistance of the smart technologies crew members could perform multiple highly specialized tasks. As a result, idle time could be eliminated, and the crew could be reduced by 80 percent. This new management paradigm became known across industries as "minimal manning."

Why didn't it work? There were many well-known trade-offs such as the ship's low survivability, which required the crew to abandon it in some cases of emergency, exposing them to significant risks. But it boiled down to unforeseen human factors. A smaller crew had more tasks to do. Hence, they had time just to react to problems without investigating and giving them due consideration. As the researchers discovered the more a crew member spent time on investigation and consideration, the lower the productivity of the crew members. Thinking can be expensive on the assembly line! To the surprise of everyone, the "hybrid" teams were not only unable to solve big problems, but they also failed to properly route tasks. One crew failed to oil the main engine causing the ship to return to base for repairs that cost the military $23 million.

The lack of expertise led to a lack of accountability. As everyone was able and tasked to do everything, no one was directly responsible and accountable for anything. Many small and big mistakes at peace time showed the dangers of combining minimal manning with smart technologies, and thus, the strategy was abandoned. Creating optimal coordination between less skilled men and smart machines is much harder than the development of autonomous machines. To achieve beneficial coordination men and machines have to be "equal" in expertise and sophistication as is the case with robotic surgery, which we will discuss later in this chapter. Augmentation of lower level skills with smart technologies can lead to more negligence on part of the employees as they begin to delegate more of the "thinking" and decision making to the machines.

As we make advances to full automation, two intermediate business models have emerged: Product-as-a-Service (PaaS) and Service-as-a-Product (SaaP).

Product-as-a-Service

Why would a traditional equipment manufacturer like GE want to become a software company? GE manufactures and sells large-scale expensive industrial equipment. But recently they changed their strategy and made a significant investment to develop the Predix software platform in an effort to become one of the largest software companies.

All industrial equipments have an expected life span. These expectations are used to forecast and plan maintenance and new sales revenues. Some machines have a longer- and others have a shorter life span than the average expected life span. All machines are built in the same way and have identical parts. Thus, the differences in their life span are due to variations in the operating conditions.

Equipment manufacturers and their customers have exactly the opposite preferences with respect to machine life span. Manufacturers want shorter life spans as this leads to more sales, and the customers want longer life spans as it reduces their capital investments. Manufacturers gain when the actual life span is less than the average expected life span, and customers gain if it is higher. Since the interests of manufacturers and customers are not aligned, there are business opportunities to monetize the gap.

Numerous innovative companies have developed specialized equipment monitoring and predictive maintenance solutions to optimize the operating conditions and beat the average machine life expectancy. Such companies charge a fraction of the equipment replacement cost for each year of extended service. Over time the manufacturers noticed that their sales cycles had become longer. The new analytics and monitoring services were in effect eroding their margins. The only way to combat this situation is by selling not the equipment but the outcomes of their products. When the customer buys the outcomes of a machine and not the machine itself, the interests of manufacturers and customers become 100 percent aligned. Since the outcomes are not dependent on the life span of the machine, the new PaaS business model eliminates the life span arbitrage opportunities that existed between manufacturers and owners.

The concept of selling the service instead of the product itself is not new. In 1962 Rolls Royce started a marketing campaign for its aircraft engines under the tagline "power by the hour."[7] This was essentially a maintenance service at fixed price per flying hour. However, in the absence of detailed operational data the problem of moral hazard arises. This is a situation when one party engages in a riskier than usual behavior knowing that another party will carry the costs if something goes wrong. Once the cost is fixed per flying hour, some operators may undertake riskier flights that increase the wear and tear of the equipment or lead to sudden breaks. The collection of detailed data solves this problem as it can demonstrate any violations of the operating conditions. Today, fleet management companies build driving profiles of the individual drivers that can pinpoint how sudden acceleration or sudden breaking increases the wear and tear of tires and other parts of the trucks and increases the cost of maintenance.

In 2017, Rolls Royce and Nor Line, a Norwegian shipping company, announced a completely new service level agreement based on big data and analytics.[8] It was announced as a new kind of a "power by the hour" agreement, as Rolls Royce had developed a complete sensor-based remote monitoring of all cargo vessels which gives them full transparency into each ship's operations and conditions. Each ship is being treated like a Check Point Cardio's remote monitored patient that we discussed in Chapter 3. The complete transparency into the ships' operations makes the fixed price fair as the manufacturer knows best how its equipment should work and be serviced.

---

[7] "'Power-by-the-Hour', a Rolls-Royce trademark, was invented in 1962 to support the Viper engine on the de Havilland/Hawker Siddeley 125 business jet. A complete engine and accessory replacement service was offered on a fixed-cost-per-flying-hour basis. This aligned the interests of the manufacturer and operator, who only paid for engines that performed well." https://rolls-royce.com/media/press-releases-archive/yr-2012/121030-the-hour.aspx (accessed December 14, 2019).

[8] World Maritime News. 2017. "Nor Lines, Rolls-Royce Ink 1st "Power-by-the-Hour" Service Agreement." https://worldmaritimenews.com/archives/220813/nor-lines-rolls-royce-ink-1st-power-by-the-hour-service-agreement/ (accessed November 12, 2019).

Service-as-a-Product

"There are many more people who want to be healthy and fit but who do not go to gyms than those who go to gyms"—Min Kim, founder and CEO of Wise Wellness (wisewellness.co.kr) told me. Kim lives in Seoul and shows me from his office window how many people do physical exercise on the sidewalks in front of their office buildings. He explains to me that these are people who find a few free minutes during their busy days, walk outside, and do a few simple exercises for 5 to 10 minutes. Some of them do it several times per day. This is so normal in Korea that pedestrians do not even pay attention to the people doing stretches, jumps, and other exercises, which we may find weird in New York.

Kim explains that people need 2.5 hours of exercise per week according to a U.S. army research paper. The physical exercises do not have to be done at once or in 30 minutes increments as we do when we go to the gym. All people need is a few minutes of moderate intensity anaerobic activity per day. There are many reasons why people do not follow this simple recommendation. Lack of motivation is the key factor for not exercising. It is also the reason why people hire personal coaches or join gym classes.

Min Kim's idea was to make these short exercises as easy and convenient to do as it seemed to be for the people who do them on the streets and in the parks of Seoul. No need for wearable devices, no trips to the gym, and no live coaches. What people got out of the various exercise devices and facilities had to be packaged as an app in the one device that no one in Seoul could live without—the smartphone.

To replace the fitness instructor the smartphone had to be able to monitor accurately what a person does, assess the intensity of the activity, track progress over time, and provide advice. Kim packaged the services provided by gyms and fitness instructors in a SaaP mobile app. To make it simple Kim focused on the five basic exercises—squats, push-ups, sit-ups, short climbs, and walking. All exercises, except walking, require visual monitoring to prevent cheating.

You may wonder if people cheat about how much they exercise. They do. I have seen many people shaking their Fitbit devices vigorously to make it up to the daily steps goal. You can even purchase devices for steps faking if shaking a device is too much of an exercise. People cheat for different reasons. Some want to win contests or impress others, others want to prove that they comply with prescribed exercise routines, and many just lack the motivation to exercise but do not want to acknowledge their weakness of the will. Life coaches keep people honest. And this is exactly what Kim's app does. It recognizes the physical movements associated with each exercise, assesses their correctness, and calculates the goal achievement. Companies in Korea provide the app as part of their benefit packages to help employees stay fit and healthy.

Min Kim is not the only entrepreneur who has packaged a services-as-a-product. Software chatbots also provide services-as-products. The menless service is significantly cheaper. Min's app retails for $1.50 per month, while the average hourly rate for a fitness coach is $20. By making coaching affordable and exercise convenient, Min is driving more people to do it. Similar to location-based apps, Min's app can be used anywhere and anytime. Affordable and scalable service is at the core of the proliferation of this new technology and data-driven business model.

Opportunity Matrix for the Man-Less Business Model

The man-less business models, regardless of whether they are PaaS or SaaP, are built entirely on data and analytics. The opportunities can be mapped to two dimensions—the autonomy of the machine and the completeness of the tasks that it does. Autonomy is the degree to which the machine can make decisions without human assistance. The second dimension reflects whether the machine does the entire job by itself, or a subset of the tasks within a larger process. In the latter case, the machine is a component within a more complex system. The matrix in Figure 10.1 shows the different categories within the two dimensions.

The autonomous car and the autonomous ship will perform the entire job without human assistance. While we are not 100 percent there yet, the end goal is a completely autonomous and independent machine. A fully autonomous car will take passengers from point to point safely without a human driver, and a fully autonomous ship will complete a mission without a crew and without being operated by a remote control. The market and the monetization opportunities are huge as autonomous

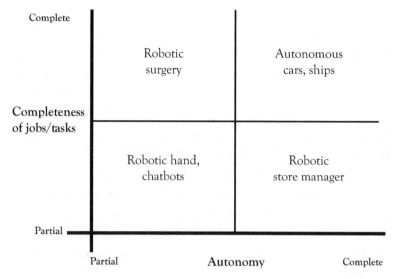

Figure 10.1 Monetization opportunity matrix: *Man-less model*

machines provide a 24/7 service without the human cost. This in turn allows companies to scale the service to many more users and deliver it at any time. Giving autonomy to machines has economic, social, and moral consequences and we are not yet fully aware of all issues or the solutions to the known issues. Since the business opportunities exist and the expected profits are huge, the transition to man-less machines will only continue to accelerate despite the concerns.

Today many retailers have deployed store robots to monitor various aspects of the retail operations. These awkward-looking "employees" can perform many tasks—monitor the available stock on the shelves, store cleanliness, security, and much more. But the store robot cannot do it all. Hence, the need for a hybrid workforce. The adoption of these machines does not depend solely on the cost savings. It will depend on how they fit with other employees and customers. Awkward machines can turn customers off and send them to more traditionally managed stores. The winners in this space will invent new human machine interaction paradigms that will make the autonomous machines more acceptable to humans.

Shadow Robot Company (shadowrobot.com) is a UK-based company that has been working for years to create the perfect robotic hand. Such technology can do many useful things. The robotic hand can pick up strawberries or roses, play ping pong, and even replace the human hand in the case of full or partial hand loss. The robotic hand has a lot of built in intelligence. Like the human hand it has not only dexterity, but also sensitivity that allows it to determine if a fruit is ripe or not, if the grip is too strong to break an object or too weak to hold it. However, the hand is only a component of a larger system. All the information collected by the hand feeds the "brain" of a larger autonomous process that completes the entire job. The same applies for chatbots as they perform limited functions within larger systems. While the robotic components do not have complete machine autonomy, as they cannot complete an entire job, their intelligence is limited to the task at hand. The monetization of components depends on the demand and adoption of larger systems and is analogous to the economics of parts suppliers in the automotive industry.

A surgical robot, like the DaVinci robot and its competitors, can perform with its mechanical arms all the tasks that a surgeon does—cutting, stitching, and so on. But despite its mechanical complexity, the robot lacks full autonomy and requires a human surgeon. I asked Dr. Stoyanov who heads the computer vision lab at the University College London to explain to me why we needed this expensive equipment in addition to the surgeon. It appears that we have added to the cost of the surgeon the cost of the robot and raised the overall cost of surgery. He told me that there were many reasons. I asked for the simplest benefit that anyone unskilled in the art of robotic surgery will understand instantly.

"Imagine an open-heart surgery," he started. "It is a big opening. There is a lot of blood and exposed flesh. This invites many bacteria to feast on the patient that can cause deadly infections." I got it right away. The three small keyholes through which the robotic arms perform the surgery eliminate the banquet opportunities for the bacteria. Of course, there are other benefits such as the real-time feedback to the surgeon from the analysis of the streamed visual data that reduce deadly mistakes. In time this data and analysis will allow the surgical robot to become more autonomous. The market for augmentation of human skills with robotic equipment is as huge as the market for amplifying the human physical skills with industrial equipment that caused Ricardo's initial fascination with machines.

Today, all four quadrants are blue oceans for innovation and new business models development, and yet many people fear automation.

What Should We Be Afraid Of?

There is a lot of anxiety and social fear about automation. The topic is so broad and complex that it will take decades of research and practice to resolve it. But in general, humanity has resolved many such dilemmas in the course of action, that is, as the events occur, and not beforehand in an academic style policy discussion. From this perspective, we should take a pragmatic approach to our fears. We should be afraid of the present negative trends and not of future imaginary effects. It is the present that shapes the future, and if it takes the wrong course the negative effects are likely to occur. From this perspective, we should not fear meaningful automation; we should be afraid of meaningless automation.

The pursuit of meaningless automation starts with the digitization of activities and processes without measurable improvement the human condition, the completion of tasks, or some other outcome. As engineers try to show improvement of outcomes in failing automation projects, they frequently begin to constrain the human activity in order to improve the machine productivity. This is the situation when machines and computer programs become "prescriptive," that is, they dictate to human beings how things should be done instead of facilitating the doing of things. This can easily be seen in the case of chatbots that force us to go through a meaningless sequence of questions and answers to get to the point. Human conversations can take many paths, but chatbots often constrain us to a single path that wastes time and frustrates us. Why should I have to answer 20 questions before getting connected to a live representative?

In his book "The Glass Cage: Automation and Us," Nicholas Carr discusses at length the drawbacks of "prescriptive" automation. He summarizes the negative effects in the following way:

> The danger looming over the creative trades is that designers and artists, dazzled by the computer's superhuman speed, precision and efficiency, will constantly take it for granted that the automated way is the best way. They will ignore the tradeoffs that the

software imposes on them without considering them. They will rush down the path of least resistance, even though a little resistance, a little friction, might have brought out the best in them.[9]

New ideas and innovation come out of the friction and difficulties that we encounter as they trigger learning. The danger of meaningless automation is that by constraining the process it forces us not to learn but to submit to the machine. To avoid the Ricardo's trap, automation should inspire and force new and higher level of learning.

[9] Carr, N. 2014. *The Class Cage: Automation and Us.* New York, NY: W.W. Norton & Company Inc.

PART III
The Analytics of Growth

Information is the oil of the 21st century, and analytics is the combustion engine.

—Peter Sondergaard, Executive Vice President,
Gartner Research & Advisory

The future belongs to those who see possibilities before they become obvious.

—John Scully, former CEO of Apple Inc.

CHAPTER 11

The Pursuit of Analytics Maturity

Today companies are racing to build analytics departments. The demand for qualified people is so strong that 46 percent of chief information officers (CIOs) reported skills shortages despite offering high salaries.[1] Why does everybody think that analytics is the new money-making secret? Why should this even surprise us? Isn't it the case that analytics has always played a key role in business?

Arithmetic and accounting were invented to make business better. In 1494, an Italian polymath Luca Pacioli published a book *Summa de arithmetica, geometria, proportioni et proportionalita (Summary of arithmetic, geometry, proportions and proportionality)*. The mathematics in it was not groundbreaking, but it contained a section on double-entry bookkeeping. Luca Pacioli was a pragmatic genius for whom the math was a means to an end. Hence, he discussed arithmetic, algebra, and geometry as means to arrive at a complete view of the business through the method of double-entry accounting.

It remains a mystery what sparked the idea of this counterintuitive record keeping method that many business students today have a hard time understanding and learning. This invention has transformed business management and has inspired the development of numerous software technologies. Even poets admired the logical structure and the power of double-entry accounting:

---

[1] Woodie. A. 2019. "What's Driving Data Science Hiring in 2019." *Datanami.* https://datanami.com/2019/01/30/whats-driving-data-science-hiring-in-2019/ (accessed November 12, 2019).

Whilst I could not think of any man whose spirit was, or needed to be, more enlarged than the spirit of a genuine merchant. What a thing it is to see the order which prevails throughout his business! By means of this he can at any time survey the general whole, without needing to perplex himself in the details. What advantages does he derive from the system of book-keeping by double entry? It is among the finest inventions of the human mind; every prudent master of a house should introduce it into his economy. (Johann Wolfgang von Goethe)[2]

For Goethe the brilliance of double-entry accounting was in its ability to show the whole picture without cluttering it with unnecessary details. A businessperson could instantly assess the health of the business, the breakdown of sales, costs, margins, and profits, without having to look at the individual transactions. In contrast, a single-entry accounting system contains nothing else but transaction details recorded in a long ledger.

In reality, business history shows an insatiable appetite for more data and deeper interest in the details. Activity-Based Costing, known also as the ABC of business, breaks down tasks and activities to the most minute details to get a more fine-grained picture of production and service costs. Furthermore, businesses were not just interested in the historical facts contained in the accounting systems. They also wanted to leverage the collected data to predict and forecast events, outcomes, and revenues. Scientifically minded managers observed patterns and relationships in the historical data and formulated theories on how to use this knowledge to improve future outcomes.

One such manager invented a method for predicting beer quality based on the amount of soft resins in the hops. He saw it as very beneficial not just for the beer industry but in general for every manufacturer. Despite the company's policy prohibiting employee publications, he submitted it to a journal as a semi-scholarly article under the pseudonym of Student. The article lacked a mathematical proof for the method and, thus, was largely ignored by the scientific community until a prominent

---

[2] von Goethe, J.W. 2019. "Goethe's Works, Vol. 5: Wilhelm Meister's Travels, A Romance; Elective Affinities" (Classic Reprint) Paperback.

statistician Ronald Aylmer Fisher[3] provided the mathematical proof. The T-test, as it is known today, was empirically derived by the self-taught statistician William Sealy Gosset while working for the Guinness brewery and has been extensively used in many industries.

The desire for more data and deeper insights is natural because data makes decisions fact based instead of gut based. There is an ongoing debate in science and business about the benefits of gut feeling versus analysis for decision making. Gut decisions are prone to errors, whereas analysis leads to paralysis. Neither argument is conclusive, but what is known is that we lean on the gut when we lack information. Hence, more information eliminates the doubts of the gut. And yet, information is often intentionally or unintentionally ignored. Sometimes businesspeople are overoptimistic or overconfident and ignore the facts. Bright sidedness,[4] the winner effect,[5] and different cognitive biases shut down our reasoning even in the presence of information. We also ignore the facts when they overwhelm us.

In 2005, we presented oncologists with big data patient profiles and asked them to determine the disease stage. A big data patient profile is essentially a general ledger of every health care transaction payed by an insurance company. Every test, every procedure, every hospital, or physician visit is recorded in the ledger. The transactional profile of each patient can be 300 pages or more of raw data. This information is quite different from the 500 words summary profiles that doctors typically see. Most oncologists made mistakes when interpreting the transactional profiles. When reviewing the errors, they acknowledged that the information was too much. They zeroed in a few data points but missed the significance of others. Ian Ayres, professor of law at Yale University and author of the book "Super Crunchers," explains this limitation of the human brain:

---

[3] Holmes, C. 2019. "The Genius at Guinness and his Statistical Legacy." *The Conversation.* http://theconversation.com/the-genius-at-guinness-and-his-statistical-legacy-93134 (accessed November 12, 2019).

[4] Ehrenreich, B. 2009. *Bright-sided: How the Relentless Promotion of Positive Thinking Has Undermined America.* New York, NY: Henry Holt Books.

[5] Robertson, I.H. 2012. *The Winner Effect: The Neuroscience of Success and Failure.* New York, NY: Thomas Dunne Books.

We tend to defer to experiential experts when some process is really complicated. But when there are more than say 5 causal factors, human experts tend to do a very bad job at correctly assigning the correct weights to what causes what.[6]

To Goethe's credit, we need to save the brain from being overwhelmed by too much detail. Hence, the desire for systems and technologies that analytically augment the human brain and supply it with a picture that allows the brain to focus only on the relevant information like the double-entry accounting method does. Intelligent analytics systems filter out the noise of irrelevant details instead of arbitrarily ignoring them as people do when overwhelmed by information.

Opportunity Monetization Matrix for Data and Analytics

There is a linear relationship between the depth of data that companies collect and the sophistication of the analytics methods that they need to process this data for monetization. The data depth is determined by dimensionality and granularity of the data. Dimensionality reflects the number of descriptive attributes that characterize each business transaction, event, product, part, and so on, that is captured and stored as raw data. For example, a real estate property can have many attributes such as ownership, zoning, land use, condition, number and type of rooms, financing, taxes, and much more. In fact, such attributes are frequently sold as data products that enrich other data to improve its access and analyze. Wand, Inc. (wandinc.com) sell product enrichment data that ensures that e-commerce sites deliver optimal user experience through complex attribute-based filtering and search. ESRI (esri.com), the mapping company, sells more than 15,000 demographic, psychographic, and socioeconomic variables, each having hundreds of attributes, to improve the analysis of geospatial information. Having these attributes allows an

---

[6] "Super Crunching" Interview with Ian Ayers, September 11, 2007, *Financial Times* https://ft.com/content/e5527304-5af9-11dc-8c32-0000779fd2ac (accessed December 14, 2019).

analyst to extract deeper insights for every slice of the world's map. The more facets we can look through, the more informed decisions we can make.

Granularity determines the time intervals at which data is being analyzed. Yearly, quarterly, monthly, and daily reports are used to track performance and goal achievement. Companies used to be run on monthly and quarterly reports, but today's Twitter and instant messenger culture make even the daily reports old news. Breaking news spreads instantly both in politics and within organizations. Good and bad news break in the digital grapevine before the reports can even be generated. Rumors about bad quarterly results or new competitor actions break out before any formal announcement. Not only our expectations about the timing of information have changed, but the pace of business has changed too. Windows of opportunities have shortened. Flash sales sites like Gilt.com have turned fashion retail into happenstance and consequently hooked people to their instant messages. As a result, traditional managerial decision making is moving closer and closer to real time, whereas decision automation can only be done in real time.

The increasing data dimensionality and granularity created big data. Even though it is humans who wanted and created big data, it is humanly impossible to analyze it with a pencil, paper, calculator, and spreadsheet. It is humanly impossible to comprehend the many dimensions, as Ian Ayres points out, and humanly impossible to see data collected at 20 or 40 MHz sampling rate, which is 20,000 or 40,000 data points per second. In the era of big dimensional and granular data, human intuitions and analytical skills must be augmented with the right tools and methods to enable the utilization of this new resource.

The monetization opportunity matrix in Figure 11.1 shows how the accumulation of data transformed it in what Clive Humby, the British mathematician who established Tesco's Clubcard loyalty program, calls "the new crude oil."[7] Clive's analogy is quite relevant as both crude oil and raw big data have practically no value until processed, and that is what sophisticated analytics does to data.

---

[7] Fagden, J. 2019. "Yes, Data Is the New Oil." *Data and Analytics Blog*, http:// bulletinhealthcare.com (accessed November 23, 2019).

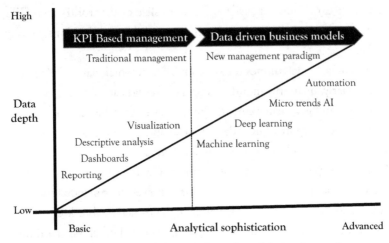

Figure 11.1 **Data growth drives analytical sophistication and monetization:** *Data depth vs analytics breadth*

Today's most hyped analytics technologies—machine learning and neural networks—are not new. Linear regression was invented in 1870 and neural networks in 1943. What is driving their adoption on a massive scale is the digitization process that turns everything from letters, to voice, to video and images into raw data that feeds these algorithms. While traditional business analysis focused on measurement, reporting, and visualization of performance metrics such as sales, shipments, and so on, the new approaches process raw data into digital "finished goods." Classification algorithms turn raw images and streaming video into well-organized digital catalogues that can be repurposed or sold in many ways. Algorithms that predict events such as machine failures deliver equipment "inspections" without mechanical inspection and human intervention. Decision automation and artificial intelligence (AI) runs cars, warehouses, and much more. The analytical algorithms perform tasks that allow companies to make money. Bitcoin mining does that literally as the miners get rewarded with Bitcoins for cracking algorithms to unlock more coins into the system. The digital gold rush has as strong of a pull as the California gold rush. It is estimated that 300,000 gold seekers immigrated to California in the 1850s. Today, Slush Pool (slushpool.com) lists 260,000 active digital miners, whereas other sites estimate this number to be over

1,000,000[8] proving that the alchemy of data and analytics can produce real money out of abstract ideas.

Traditional reporting does not perform tasks nor can turn abstract ideas into money. Reporting, descriptive analysis, and visualizations are used to manage the business. Are the business objectives and goals being met and if not, why? Thus, reporting, like accountings, is a cost center. But big data and advanced analytics are sources for monetization. Humanly curated image libraries tend to be small as their creation is labor intensive and expensive. Machine curation allows for expanding the libraries and delivering real-time packaged content for a fee. Stock trading predictions are signals that can be packaged as data products and sold to institutional or individual investors as AlgorithmicTrading.net does. Hence, companies are aggressively maturing their analytics to use the data not just to manage the business but also to generate revenues. The more task oriented the analytics are, the higher the monetization opportunity. Highly dimensional data with low granularity coupled with sophisticated analytics transformed the purpose, the utilization, and monetization of data.

Why Companies Develop Decision-Styles Cultures and Systems

Different analytic methods evolve because new data types emerge. Different analytics systems and platforms are built to support new decision-making styles. The intuitive versus the logical/rational decision styles feature prominently in all personality tests. But why do companies create cultures and build systems to support different decision styles? The simple answer is that better decisions lead to better business results. While this is true, it is not the complete answer.

---

[8] "How Many Bitcoin Miners Are There? Slushpool has about 200,000 miners. They have 12% of the network hash rate. Assuming all pools have similar numbers, there are likely to be over 1,000,000 unique individuals mining bitcoins." https://buybitcoinworldwide.com/how-many-bitcoins-are-there/ (accessed November 23, 2019).

Companies need to standardize the decision-making process to ensure consistency and reduce risk. Imagine what it takes to manage a few hundred loan originators for second-hand car dealerships? Some loan originators are intuitive, and others are rational decision makers. How do you ensure that they assess risks correctly and price the loans based on the risk that the dealer may default on the loan? This was the biggest challenge of the CIO of a financial services company that provided commercial loans to second-hand car dealerships.

When I met her in 2010, the story intrigued me instantly. The market for second-hand cars had become famous in game theory because of a paper that won a Nobel Prize. "The Market for Lemons,"[9] as the title of the paper is, describes a situation of information asymmetry. One side of the transaction, the seller, has complete information about the quality of the car. But the dealer can also withhold some of this information from the buyer. Hence, the asymmetry—one party of the transaction knows more than the other and can use this to get a better deal for himself. The sly second-hand car dealer knows that sooner or later the buyer will find the truth and will feel like he has chewed on a lemon. Searching Google for images of "second-hand car salesmen" returns a massive number of images created intentionally to portray them as cunning, manipulative, and eager to profit from human misery.

As the CIO explained to me, this perception of the second-hand car salesman is mostly wrong. Second-hand car dealerships are small businesses working hard to compete with the large new car dealerships that also sell pre-owned certified vehicles. The owners/managers do not have business training and frequently overestimate the market and the risks when they finance their inventory. Thus, many of them default on their loans.

Sometimes, a friend had asked them to find them a luxury car on a deal, to purchase the car at an auction, make extra profit, and decide that this may be a good market segment. As they upscale the cars on the lot, the more expensive cars take longer to sell, and their cash flow suffers. Other times, they decide to improve the lot and invest in pavement,

---

[9] Arkerlof, G. 1970. "The Market for Lemons: Quality Uncertainty and the Market Mechanism." *Quarterly Journal of Economics. The MIT Press* 84, no. 3, 488–500. https://doi.org/10.2307/1879431 (accessed November 12, 2019).

fences, and other amenities, but the volume of sales does not support the decorative expenditures. As she explained to me, the dealers genuinely believe and intend to do well when making these changes. And so are also the loan originators who develop friendly relationships with the dealership owners and want to help them to do well. The path to bankruptcy is paved by good intentions as compassion and optimism lead to underestimation of the true financial risks.

But who wants to acknowledge that their intuitions and good intentions lead to bad decisions? The company had ongoing open discussions whether financing fenced lots and other amenities leads to better sales or not without ever reaching a conclusion while writing off 20 to 30 percent of the loans. According to the CIO the only way to resolve the debates and solve the problem was by establishing a decision style and a culture of fact-based decision making. Implementing a new decision support system with a predictive risk score based on the sales history and the cumulative risk based on the total unpaid loans was not trivial to implement. Unlike the big car dealerships that have a single credit line, second-hand car dealership financing is more like microloans financing because each car purchase loan is a separate origination. Even more difficult was to mandate the use of the risk score by the loan originators as culture cannot be forced upon employees with an order. Since a risk score is just a guiding benchmark, the loan originators can either ignore or take it seriously, and the disbelievers tend to ignore it. The good thing about historical data is that at some point the accumulated facts are impossible to ignore. Within a year, everyone saw that the brutal reality and the unintended consequences of financing improvements that made the lots prettier but often pushed dealers into cash flow problems and bankruptcy.

The Enterprise Analytics Stack for the Digital Economy

With the abundance of data and analytics, the analytics maturity curve is continuously incorporating a broader range of decision styles, as the graph in Figure 11.2 shows.

There are four main styles of decision making in organizations. These decision styles are not mutually exclusive. They are complimentary and

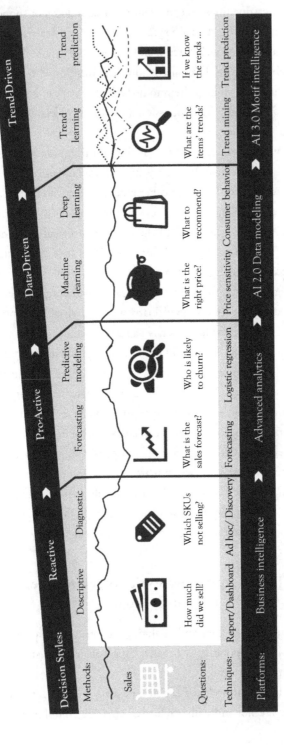

Figure 11.2 **Enterprise analytics stack for the digital economy:** *Retail example*

each style serves a different purpose and is supported by different technologies. Therefore, organizations are building stacks of analytical technologies and capabilities.

The first decision-making style has existed for centuries and is at the core of all accounting and reporting information. The reactive decision-making style looks at historical data to assess past performance. This analysis reveals either achievement or divergence from the set goals, and root cause analysis provides explanations about why things work or don't work. The reactive style informs decisions about corrective actions. The decisions about what to do are made by experts to the best of their knowledge and based on their personal experience how to align performance with goals and expectations. The reactive decision style is often compared to looking at the rearview mirror. But this comparison is false. History is necessary, and forward looking and predictive systems need even a more fine-grained history to learn from in order to make predictions. The rearview benchmarks measure the business health over time in a consistent way. Hence, nearly 100 percent of business organizations globally have deployed Business Intelligence platforms and nearly 25 percent of the workforce uses these technologies to measure performance.

The proactive decision style aims to enable action before events occur. Sales forecasts are typically done in order to measure whether progress is being made to meet the forecast. Forecasts are generated using statistical methods that extrapolate future projections from past performance data. Thus, managers do not have to wait for the end of the quarter report to see the budgeted versus actual sales. They can make decisions based on deviations from the forecast. Predictions are also used to manage customer churn. By predicting the likely attrition of some customers, managers can design and provide incentives to retain them as it is cheaper to retain existing customers than to acquire new ones.

Today, all machine learning, deep learning, and AI involves prediction. When an algorithm decides which category an image or a text belongs to, or when it classifies a medical condition of a patient, or when it autocompletes a sentence in an e-mail, it actually makes a prediction. These sophisticated task-oriented AI algorithms both fascinate and scare us because for centuries we have thought of tasks as uniquely human activities. We are so possessive of our tasks that whenever someone interferes with the work of another human being, they feel like this person is stepping on their toes.

The data-driven decision style leverages the machine learning and deep learning technologies to do tasks, such as classifying information, or deliver processed information, such as a recommended diagnosis, to decision makers. The advantage of these systems is that they can sift through a lot more data than we can and deliver insights and knowledge very fast, accurately, and on schedule. Image and video interpretation systems that can identify "what, where, and who" can tell stories. On construction sites such systems are used to increase the safety of the workers by "watching" and telling the stories to management. Such safety stories were previously anecdotal and incomplete—whatever the foreman saw and remembered. Data driven makes the stories factual and reliable, but as a decision-making style it is possible only through technology augmentation.

And just when we thought that machine learning and deep learning are the solution to all analytics and AI problems, DARPA, the Defense Advanced Research Projects Agency of the United States Department of Defense that is responsible for the development of emerging technologies, made a startling announcement that it will invest over $2 billion in new research projects on a next-generation AI, or as they called it AI 3.0:

> Past DARPA AI investments facilitated the advancement of "first wave" (rule based) and "second wave" (statistical learning based) AI technologies. DARPA-funded R&D enabled some of the first successes in AI, such as expert systems and search, and more recently has advanced machine learning algorithms and hardware. DARPA is now interested in researching and developing "third wave" AI theory and applications that address the limitations of first and second wave technologies.[10]

With this announcement, it seems that the we are just starting to explore the real possibilities.

---

[10] Grant Number: DARPA-PA-18-02 Program Announcement (PA) Artificial Intelligence Exploration (AIE).

While the data-driven approach allows us to act on deeper insights or previously unavailable knowledge, the trend-driven decision-making style allows businesses to react to the ever-changing trends and patterns in business operations. The trends-based approach pushes the analytical boundaries in two important aspects. First, most statistical approaches assume that time in these models is stationary, that is, the models assume that events will repeat themselves in a similar fashion over time. But as one data scientist who runs a business pointed out to me: "Time is not stationary. We pay managers to change things over time." Second, the trend-driven approach disaggregates the analytics. All analysis from accounting to statistics summarizes the data or extrapolates the representative patterns. The trend-driven approach identifying microtrends at the unit level—the individual machine, patient, Stock Keeping Unit sales, and much more. This is a positive "micromanagement" as it creates new opportunities to manage outcomes, save costs, and optimize revenues, which we will discuss in the next chapter.

CHAPTER 12

Beating the Averages With Trends AI

In July 1982 Jay Gould, the renowned evolutionary anthropologist, decided not to succumb to the hard facts of medical statistics. He was diagnosed with abnormal mesothelioma, a deadly cancer caused by exposure to asbestos. Since the doctor refused to tell him the life expectancy for his cancer, he did the research himself at the medical library at Harvard. The median life expectancy was merely eight months.

"So that's why they didn't give me anything to read," he thought. His second thought after the initial shock is quite unusual for someone in his condition, "Then my mind started to work again, thank goodness."[1] This marks the beginning of his rejection to accept the median and the average as a meaningful measure of cancer survival rates. Digging deeper in the medical research, he realized that countless number of factors such as age, class, wealth, socioeconomic status, demographics, attitudes, and many more, contributed significantly to a shorter or longer than eight month's life expectancy.

He objects to using the median and the average for communicating life expectancy of uncurable diseases because the positive attitude of terminally ill patients plays a crucial role in increasing the treatment effects. But statistical prognosis is usually a killer of positive attitude because people who are not versed in the science of statistics inevitably misinterpret the message. As he points out:

What does "median mortality of eight months" signify in our vernacular? I suspect that most people, without training in statistics, would read such a statement as "I will probably be dead in eight

---

[1] Gould, S.J. 2013. "The Median Isn't the Message." *AMA Journal of Ethics*.

months"—the very conclusion that must be avoided, both because this formulation is false, and because attitude matters so much.[2]

The problem with measures of statistical tendencies, like the median and the average, is that they are taken as hard facts, while the variation around them is ignored. But it should be exactly the opposite. Variation is the fact of life, while the median and the average are just artifacts providing an inexact representation of a much more complex reality. As an evolutionary biologist, Jay Gould knew that variation is the "irreducible essence of nature." He died in 2002, 20 years after his diagnosis, from a completely different disease.

To be fair, doctors are quite aware that the averages are misleading. I took a stress test a year ago. I asked the nurse how long it would take to raise my pulse to the required 165 beats per minute by running on the treadmill. To my surprise she said that she didn't know. How was this possible when she had been doing this for 25 years? "What about on average?" I asked, to which she replied, "There is no average. Every heart is different." When I told the story to a scientist who works with cardiologists, he told me that when doctors hear statistical quotes, they often tell an old joke: "The average patient temperature in the hospital is normal. Half of the patients have high fever and the other half are dead."

Not only every heart is different, but so is every individual. Norman and Norma are two alabaster statues representing the average man and woman in America. They were created by the artist Abram Belskie and the obstetrician-gynecologist Robert Latou Dickinson in 1943, based on the average measurements of 15,000 men and women between the ages of 21 and 25.[3] The Cleveland Health Museum purchased the statues and sponsored a contest in 1945 to find women in Ohio whose body shape and measurements closely matched the statue of Norma. The museum offered $100 to women to measure their hips, bust, neck width, wrist circumference, and so on. About 3,863 women entered the contest but to the surprise of everyone less than 40 came close to matching the dimensions

[2] Gould, S.J. 2013. "The Median Isn't the Message." *AMA Journal of Ethics.*

[3] Cambers, D.S. 2004. "The Law of Averages 1: Normman and Norma: Looking for Mr. and Mrs. America." *Cabinet Magazine,* no. 15.

of Norma. This is a mere one percent—a dismal accuracy. If one were to use the average Norma as a guide to mass manufacture women's wear, the results would be devastating.

Tod Rose, author of the book "The End of Averages: How We Succeed in a World That Values Sameness,"[4] shows how no one can be average when the mix of all attributes that make an individual are considered. In the book he is making the case against "averagiarism" and the social consequences when we strive to be average. In trying to do so, people lose the dignity of their individuality.

The problem exits in business, too, despite the pervasive use of averages in almost all reports. Sam Savage, a Stanford economist, points out that decisions based on averages are wrong on average.[5] He illustrates the point with a joke about a statistician who drowned in a river that is on average three feet deep. The river is six inches deep near the banks and eight feet deep in the center. The average is meaningless in this case.

The "flaw of averages," as Sam Savage calls it, can be illustrated with a simple example from crypto trading. Many crypto traders have switched to pattern-based trading precisely to avoid averages. Let us look at two patterns—"double tops" and "double bottoms," as shown in Figure 12.1:

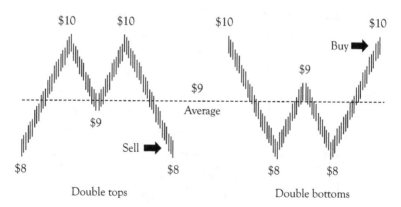

Figure 12.1 The flaw of averages: *Equities trading example*

[4] Rose, T. 2016. *The End of Average: How We Succeed in a World That Values Sameness.* HarperCollins Publishers.

[5] Savage, S. 2002. "The Flaw of Averages." *Harvard Business Review*, November Issue.

The two shapes are identical. One is a "W" and the other an inverted "W." The Double Bottoms is a buy signal, whereas the Double Tops is a sell signal. The average is the same—$9. If a trader makes a decision based on the average of $9, the decision will be as good as the toss of a coin. There is not enough information in the single number about the direction in which the market is going. The longer and the more complex the underlying trend is, the less useful a single average number is for making decisions.

The example applies to every industry and every measurable process. How would a retail marketer make campaign decisions based on monthly averages without knowing whether sales are trending upward or downward? The old joke that half of the marketing spend works, but no one knows which half, reflects the reality that decisions based on averages are only as good as a coin toss. An item that starts selling low, but raises quickly, will produce the same average as an item that starts selling high but decreases rapidly. The direction and the shape of the trend matters. Averages are accurate only when the trends are constant, which happens neither in nature nor in business. When the data fluctuates, the averages are poor guides in decision making.

If the averages are such a poor guide for decision making, why do we invest so much in business intelligence and analytics technologies that process data and compute averages? And why do we make decisions based on the averages? It was practical necessity. People do not have the time and the resources to look at granular data. How can a retail store manager look at the individual sales trends of all items sold in the store? How can the marketer look at all stores and all items to select candidates for promotions? If your retail chain has 1,000 stores and 10,000 SKUs, this will require analyzing 10 million individual sales patterns. This is the curse of dimensionality. The more information we collect on individually monitored items, the more knowledge we have and the more accurate decisions we can make, but it is impossible to sift through all this detail. It is also financially impossible, as the analysis will require an army of highly paid analysts. As the head of analytics in a large U.S. bank told me, it takes a very long time for the analysts to look at the data and report the trends of each product within each branch. Hence, it is more practical to look at the category level, that is, at the average for all products that fall in some predefined group.

As we already saw without understanding the underlying trends, decisions based on averages can be only as good as decisions based on gut feelings. Many professionals quickly release that and opt to rely on their gut entirely. Instead of pivoting data in Excel, professionals often rely on their observations about what is happening in the business. The gut uses information that cannot be extracted easily from the haystack of data.

The curse of dimensionality manifests itself both in nature and in business. Yet every business strives to overcome it and beat the averages to produce higher returns and higher customer satisfaction. The stock market does not reward average performers, and customers migrate to competitors who exceed the average expectations. Moving beyond the averages requires granular analytics at the individual unit level and scalable business processes for unit level customization.

In 2016 Adidas launched its "robot-powered, on-demand sneaker factory."[6] It is a miniature, in-store factory. Customers step in a box for a body scan. Complex analytics process the scan and generate a custom-tailored ergonomic design for completely personalized sneakers that are instantly manufactured in the store. The store factory is still a concept, but it marks the beginning of a very significant transformation of the industrial manufacturing process since its inception in the 1800s. Manufacturing is moving away from mass production to analytical craftsmanship at scale. Custom-tailored clothing and footwear were traditionally handmade and expensive. Analytical craftsmanship leverages new types of smart technologies to make custom-tailored products both at scale and at affordable prices. The benefits of custom-tailored footwear go far beyond the company's profits. Consumers get not only extra comfort but also reduced health care risks because of the built-in custom orthotics. Society benefits from a reduction in health care costs as custom shoes alleviate many of the common foot issues which drive physician visits and treatments.

As the Adidas concept shows, variety presents new opportunities that can be monetized if we can understand and act on the individual patterns captured in data. It has been the dream of merchandisers and marketers

[6] Wiener, A. 2017. "Inside Adidas' Robot-Powered, On-Demand Sneaker Factory." *Wired*.

to be able to create segments of one, of manufacturers to offer highly customized products, and of health care professionals to offer personalized medication. The barrier was the time and resources required to analyze and understand the individual unit. It would be too costly for Adidas to put certified podiatrist at all stores and the individual exams would be too time consuming.

New types of shape-based artificial intelligence (AI) mimics how the human brain processes information to learn and form expectations about the future, that is, plan and predict. The human brain processes vast amounts of sensory data and makes fine-grained distinctions. We instantly recognize different faces, but more generally, the brain instantly assesses the differences between the shapes of objects. In his book "How the Mind Works," Steven Pinker states:

> When we recognize an object's shape, we are acting as pure geometers, surveying the distribution of matter in space and finding the closes match in memory.[7]

According to him people remember about 10,000 different shapes. When presented with a new object, the brain searches through the stored shapes, identifies a match, and draws conclusions based on the closeness of the perceived shape to the stored shape. The brain does not perform a pixel by pixel matching as the shapes of similar objects in the world are never exactly the same. They should be similar enough for the brain to recognize the object. Researchers performed a clever experiment to identify this mental process. They showed individuals different shapes and asked them to commit them to memory. Then they asked the individuals to identify the previously seen shapes within a new set of shapes. However, the researchers rotated the previously known shapes in the new set. It took the individuals longer to recognize the shapes that were rotated. The more complex the shape and the larger the rotation angle, the longer it took the individuals to match the shapes. The process of mental rotation indicated to the researchers that the brain matches visual shapes

---

[7] Pinker, S. 2009. *How the Mind Works*. W.W. Norton & Company, Inc.

against mental images of shapes. Why should this surprise us when this is exactly what cardiologists do when they read ECG data. They compare the shapes in the ECG recordings to known pathology patterns that they have memorized.

Shapes are a very powerful source of knowledge. They are also very easy to learn. As the brain does mental comparisons it recognizes what it already knows, but it also recognizes what it does not know and commits it to memory as new knowledge. Shape intelligence, also known as motif intelligence, is a powerful method to understand variety in nature and in business, and to move away from the constraints of the averages. It is a new approach that unlike traditional machine learning does not require a lot of historical data to train the machines. Finding enough historical data to implement machine learning is a challenge for business today, as a few organizations have enough data with sufficient quality to produce accurate decision support models. On the other hand, motif intelligence requires just a few observations to start using it to monitor and predict outcomes. Motif intelligence is at the core of AI 3.0, and the good news is that shapes exist in every time series data that we collect from monitoring devices and business processes. With more sensors installed than grass seeds on the planet, we can capture in time series data the DNA of every phenomenon. But how does it help us make decisions and beat the averages?

We humans communicate with words. Each word is a unique sequence of letters and sounds, and each sequence has a distinct meaning to us. We recognize words instantly, or if we don't, we add them to our personal vocabulary. What does Google do? When we search for words, Google finds matching sequences of letters and presents them to us. If there are spelling mistakes, Google assesses the difference and if it is not too big it shows the misspelled word too. Like the brain, it is doing similarity matching. Machines and sensors that track processes, events, activities, and behaviors communicate not with words, but via the shapes in the captured time series data. The ECG signal contains both normal beats and pathologies. Recognizing the different shapes representing normal and abnormal heart beats allows physicians to diagnose patients. Vibration sensors that monitor industrial equipment generate between 20,000 and 40,000 data points per second. Within this data there are distinct sequences that may scream "attention!" Meaningful patterns are like words signaling to domain experts what needs to be done to make improvements in each individually monitored unit.

Motif intelligence mimics how the eye and the brain work together to identify and recognize meaningful shapes. Only business professionals can give meaning to the shapes in their domain data. The engineer, the merchandiser, the cardiologists, and so on, all know what a meaningful pattern is. If they encounter a new one, they investigate it and when it is fully understood, it becomes a meaningful motif. Once knowledge is gained, search makes it easy to monitor and predict at the very granular level, that is, at the unit level, regardless of how many millions of units are being monitored. Search also eliminates the need for complex modeling. It is a common misconception that machines learn on their own. In traditional machine learning, training an algorithm to recognize a "cat" in pictures requires thousands of carefully selected and labeled "cat" images. Like humans, machines require training to learn but are less efficient at it. Like the mental images in the brain, search for meaningful motifs allows professionals to pull slightly varying shapes representing the same thing from tremendous volumes of data. Whether there are many or just a few similar cases, we can find them. Like we instantly recognize a face that we have not seen for a long time, so we can pull a rare occurrence.

With AI 3.0 we gain the power to learn and know very granular patterns, also called microtrends. But what does it mean to manage by microtrends rather than by Key Performance Indicators (KPIs) and averages? The idea of trend-based decision making is not new. In fact, there is a well-known saying in the financial markets that "the trend is your friend." Quants in the financial industry are looking everywhere for novel ideas and methods on how to detect early signals of trend changes. One example is the Vortex indicator[8] inspired by the work of Viktor Schauberger[9] on the flow of water in rivers. The idea behind the Vortex indicator is that

---

[8] Fairly, A. 2018. "Understand Vortex Indicator Trading Strategies." Updated February 21, 2018, https://investopedia.com/articles/active-trading/072115/understand-vortex-indicator-trading-strategies.asp

[9] Ovesen, M. 2019. *"Who was Viktor Shauberger"* http://vortex-world.org/viktorschauberger.htm (accessed November 18, 2019).

the movements in the financial markets resemble and can be modeled as the vortex motions in water. Spotting microtrends early, either algorithmically or just by observing the trading time series patterns, creates opportunities for profitable actions.

Microtrends can be leveraged either in business process management or in operational monitoring. Today many businesses aspire to achieve operational cadence, that is, complete alignment of goals and resources to achieve smooth and rhythmic operations. Interestingly enough, cadence is an aspiration to achieve repeatable motifs (sequences of steps) along every business process. But can you do it without understanding the natural patterns at the most granular level? Can you align retail operations without understanding the sales patterns of every item in every store? Rhythm requires the note sheets for all instruments and musicians in the orchestra to be perfectly aligned. People notice immediately when something is out of tune. So how can businesses achieve cadence without first understanding the granular patterns of everything they sell and do? Thus, the first step starts with the analysis of the granular patterns to identify motifs (microtrends) that managers want to sustain, accelerate, or change, and use them to develop actionable strategies.

On a high level, the strategies associated with microtrends management can be analyzed along two dimensions: volatility of the trends and duration of the trends. Every business is subject to volatility and every opportunity is time sensitive. Microtrends reflect the dynamics of those two factors, and while they are discussed most often in financial markets, they are equally valid in retail, health care, hospitality, manufacturing, energy, oil and gas, and other verticals. The diagram in Figure 12.2 shows the general strategic categories for microtrend-based management of business operations.

The bread and butter of every business relies on the stable and predictable sales of a few core products. Any disruption in the sales trends of these products can have a significant and long-lasting impact on the business. Knowing the granular sales patterns of these products allows businesses to monitor for anomalies and emerging systematic changes in the sales patterns and use these as early warning signs that require attention and action. Early warning signs can occur in individual stores or for individual items and, thus, not be detected by looking at the KPIs.

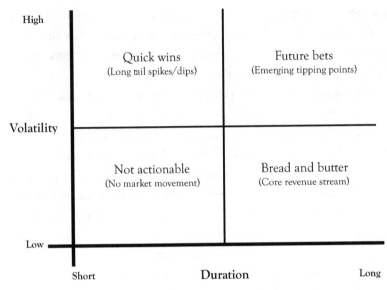

Figure 12.2 **Strategic opportunities matrix: *Micro-trends based management***

Motif intelligence will immediately show any significant change regardless of where it occurs and at what level it occurs. The bread and butter monitoring patterns form the core business portfolio of management.

Future bets are based on emerging trends that have the potential to become tipping points. Early manifestation of tipping points occurs in specific geographies and/or individual stores rather and, thus, can be easily missed in the aggregated KPIs. Identifying them early allows campaigns and promotions to test and scale the microtrend faster across all stores and geographies. Riding such microtrends allows companies to become the go to place for such trendy products or services. Future bets ensure the transition of emerging trends into bread and butter categories.

Quick wins are short-lived opportunities typically referred in retail as the long tail opportunities, that is, rarely bought items. Such items have sporadic spikes in different geographies and stores. Identifying such long tail opportunities quickly leads to better supply chain management and promotional opportunities. Occasionally, long tail opportunities turn into emerging bets, but the main benefit of knowing them is to capitalize at scale on short-lived opportunities, analogously to what arbitrageurs do in the equity markets.

Some situations just do not present an opportunity for action. If there is no movement in the stock market, there is no opportunity for trading. Knowing this information is also important in order to avoid placing bets in the stock market or overstocking on merchandise in retail.

Microtrends management allows companies to run their business more like a high-frequency trading operation, that is, recognizing and acting on opportunities in real time and making money even from small bets. In today's hypercompetitive markets, the sale of every item in every store matters for a healthy bottom line. And it applies to every opportunity in every industry. Companies have to manage on the microlevel in order to eliminate losses quickly and to increase margins. The microtrends defined for the four strategic categories form the company's portfolio of actionable business strategies, which in turn allows organizations to achieve complete cadence as resources and natural business patterns are synchronized.

How do companies leverage motifs for operational monitoring? Dictionaries explain the meaning and use of words in sentences. Like dictionaries, medical textbooks explain each cardio pathology and teach physicians how to recognize ECG patterns. As we showed earlier in this chapter, there are trading books that explain different market patterns and what can be expected when they occur. Everywhere where a process or an event is being monitored there is time series data, Excel sheets, or Power Points that visualize and explain the meaningful motifs. As sensors and monitoring devices record more and more processes and events, we will accumulate domain-specific dictionaries of meaningful motifs that will allow domain experts to better understand and manage these processes and events. These libraries of meaningful motifs will drive all managerial decisions and decision automation. If data today is an asset, the motif libraries are the vehicle to monetize this asset as they are the actionable signals that make it possible to save costs, drive revenues, and manage all outcomes. The libraries of meaningful motifs contain the organizational know-how about monetization.

As Stan Christiaens, cofounder and CTO of Collibra Inc., who turned the management of data into the main business problem and opportunity of the new digital economy and built a unicorn by providing the business tools to do that, said to me, "The best organizations figured out the ultimate control point to grow their business: data. They unlock the value ranging from measurement for better management to completely new ideas, insights, and even data products and services." Like the sequencing of DNA, the understanding of the shapes in the time series data holds the potential to create new growth opportunities and new management practices. Data and granular shape-based AI are the new steam engine.

About the Author

Dr. Rado Kotorov is a seasoned digital transformation and technology innovator with 15 years of experience as a software executive who has co-created numerous products and patented technologies. He has helped many organizations to solve today's business challenges and identify untapped revenue opportunities by using data and analytics. Dr. Rado Kotorov is a co-founder and CEO of Trendalyze, Inc., a time series intelligence and AI 3.0 platform that leverages Google-like search to discover and monitor for patterns to help organizations save costs and optimize revenues.

Index

Accumulation, 36–40
Activity-Based Costing (ABC) of
    business, 108
Adaptation as survival, 25
Adidas, 125–126
Aggregation, 36–38
Airbnb, 5, 57–58
Amazon, 32–33
Andreesen, Mark, 51
Asset density, 60
Asset-less business models, 6
    advantages of, 63–64
    challenges, 60
    monetization opportunity matrix,
        61–62
    pricing, 63
    scale and scope potential, 59–63
    sharing business models, 64–65
    short-term rental model, 61
Audible audiobook, 80
Ayres, Ian, 109

Belskie, Abram, 122
Benchmarking data products, 68
Bezos, Jeff, 36, 39
Big data patient profile, 109
Big granular data, 17
"The Black Swan" (Taleb), 52
Blockbuster, 27–29
Blockchain, 42–43
Bradenburger, Adam, 45
Buffet, Warren, 4
Business intelligence, 14
Business models, 22–23

Carr, Nicholas, 103
Change models
    business models, 22–23
    jobs, 20–22
    market competition, 23–24
Check Point Cardio, 18–20
Christiaens, Stan, 131

Coase, Ronald, 40
Cognos, 45
Cohen, Gerald, 36
Cohen, Gerry, 36
Competitive dynamics matrix, 70–71
Complete aggregation, 36–38
Concentration, 36–40
Condition-based maintenance (CBM)
    models, 21, 93–94
Cooperation, 46
Cooperative competition, 45
Coopetition, 47
"Co-opetition: A Revolution Mindset
    that Combines Competition
    and Cooperation"
    (Bradenburger and Nalebuff),
    45
Costless verification, 43

dApps, 43
Data as renewable resource, 15
Data assets monetization, 14–15
Data being an asset, 10–11
Data depth
    analytics breadth vs., 112
    dimensionality, 110–111
    granularity, 111
Data disruption, 53–54
Data-driven business model, 4, 6, 43
Data-driven companies, 5
Data-driven decision style, 118
Data first approach, 15
Data innovation, 11–13
Data products
    as business models, 67–70
    competitive dynamics matrix,
        70–71
    monetization opportunity matrix,
        73–74
    product adoption and replacement
        dynamics, 70–73
    scale and scope potential, 73–76

types of, 68
value to consumers, 76–77
Data R&D department, 14
Data scientists, 16
Decision-styles cultures and systems,
        113–115
Dickinson, Robert Latou, 122
Digital data-driven company, 50
Digital economy
    enterprise analytics stack, 115–119
    market competition rules, 47
    scale and scope, 31–33
Digital giants
    companies as, 3
    data-driven business model, 4
    reasons for, 3
Digital growth, 33
Digital opportunities
    Cambridge University research
        survey, 10–11
    data assets monetization, 14–15
    data being an asset, 10–11
    data innovation, 11–13
Digital products, 79
Digital products business models, 6
Digital supplements
    digital versions, 86–87
    life cycle supplemental add-ons,
        87–90
    monetization opportunity matrix,
        83–84
    opportunity matrix for, 83–86
    overview of, 79–83
    plastic cards, 85–86
Digital versions, 81, 86–87
Dimensionality, 110–111
Disaggregate demand, 38–39
Disaggregation
    process of, 40
    socioeconomic effects, 40–43
Double-entry accounting, 107,
        108, 110
Dresner, Howard, 14

Earning potential, 60
Ecosystem pull, 60

"The End of Averages: How We
        Succeed in a World That
        Values Sameness" (Rose), 123
Enterprise analytics stack, 115–119

Facebook, 5, 67
Financial intermediaries, 41–42
First mover advantage, 47–51
Fisher, Ronald Aylmer, 109
Flaw of averages, 123–124
Ford Model-T business model, 35, 38, 40
Franklin, Benjamin, 31
"Frequency of Use" dimension, 73–74

Game theory, 46
Gates, Bill, 36
"The Glass Cage: Automation and
        Us" (Carr), 103
Goethe, Johann Wolfgang von, 108
Google, 5, 49, 67, 127
Google maps, 74–75
Gosset, William Sealy, 109
Gould, Jay, 121, 122
Granularity, 111

Habit replacement loop, 71
Habit Stability dimension, 70
Harari, Yuval, 19
Heart-related sudden death, 18–20
"How the Mind Works" (Pinker), 126
Humby, Clive, 111

Jobs, 20–22

Kim, Min, 99
Kindle books, 80–81

Laney, Doug, 10
Lifecycle adaptation, 88
Life cycle monetization matrix, 88
Life cycle supplemental add-ons,
        87–90
Lyft, 5, 6

Malthus, Thomas, 91
Man-less business models, 6

condition-based maintenance
  system, 93, 94
lack of accountability, 96
marginal rate of technical
  substitution, 92
meaningless automation, 103–104
monetization opportunity matrix,
  101
opportunity matrix for, 100–103
overview of, 91–96
Product-as-a-Service, 97–98
rate of substation, 95
rate of technological evolution, 95
Service-as-a-Product, 99–100
Marginal rate of technical
  substitution, 92
Market competition, 23–24
Market competition rules
  first mover advantage, 47–51
  "The Winner Takes It All" (song),
    51–53
Meaningless automation, 103–104
Microtrend-based management,
  129–130
  high-frequency trading operation, 131
  key performance indicators, 128
  motifs for operational monitoring,
    131
  strategic opportunities matrix,
    129–130
Mill, James, 91
Miniaturization, 71
Monetization opportunity matrix, 61–62
  asset-less business models, 61–62
  data products, 73–74
  digital supplements, 83–84
  lifecycle adaptation, 88
  man-less business model, 101
Motif intelligence, 127–128

Nalebuff, Barry, 45
"Need to Use" dimension, 71
Netflix, 28–29
NJTransit app, 76
North, Douglass, 41

Opportunity matrix, man-less
  business models, 100–103
Opportunity monetization matrix,
  110–113

PaaS. See Product-as-a-Service
Pacioli, Luca, 107
Path dependency, 28
Personal health apps, 75
Physical assets, 4
  accumulation of, 63
Physical assets-driven economy, 50
Pinker, Steven, 126
Pinterest, 5
Predictive data products, 68
Pricing, 63
"The Principles of Political Economy
  and Taxation" (Ricardo), 92
Product-as-a-Service (PaaS), 97–98
Product-less business models, 6

Reporting, 113
Ricardo, David, 91
Rose, Tod, 123

SaaP. See Service-as-a-Product
Savage, Sam, 123
Scale and scope
  asset-less business models, 59–63
  data products, 73–76
  in digital economy, 31–33
  digital growth, 33
  in traditional economy, 29–30
Schauberger, Viktor, 128
Service-as-a-Product (SaaP), 99–100
Service-less business models, 6
Shape intelligence, 126, 127
Sharing economy model, 58
Smith, Adam, 40, 91
"Specificity" dimension, 73
Strategic opportunities matrix,
  129–130
Subscription-based business
  model, 28
Sudden cardio-related death, 18–20

"The Winner Takes It All" (song), 51–53
Traditional assets-driven company, 50
Traditional economics, 35
Traditional economy, scale and scope,
        29–30
Transaction cost
    affecting job market, 40–43
    economics, 40
Type of asset, 60

Uber, 5, 6, 7, 41, 57–58

Van Dam, Stephen, 68

Walmart, 14
Walton, Sam, 14
WebFOCUS, 45
Weiner, Eric, 83
World Wide Web, 5

OTHER TITLES IN THE BIG DATA, BUSINESS ANALYTICS, AND SMART TECHNOLOGY COLLECTION

- *Highly Effective Marketing Analytics* by Mu Hu
- *Business Analytics, Volume II* by Amar Sahay
- *New World Technologies* by Errol S. van Engelen
- *Introduction to Business Analytics* by Majid Nabavi and David L. Olson
- *Business Analytics, Volume I* by Amar Sahay
- *Location Analytics for Business* by David Z. Beitz
- *Data Mining Models, Second Edition* by David L. Olson
- *World Wide Data* by Alfonso Asensio
- *Analytics Boot Camp* by Linda Herkenhoff
- *Big Data War* by Patrick H. Park

Announcing the Business Expert Press Digital Library

Concise e-books business students need for classroom and research

This book can also be purchased in an e-book collection by your library as

- a one-time purchase,
- that is owned forever,
- allows for simultaneous readers,
- has no restrictions on printing, and
- can be downloaded as PDFs from within the library community.

Our digital library collections are a great solution to beat the rising cost of textbooks. E-books can be loaded into their course management systems or onto students' e-book readers.
The **Business Expert Press** digital libraries are very affordable, with no obligation to buy in future years. For more information, please visit **www.businessexpertpress.com/librarians**. To set up a trial in the United States, please email **sales@businessexpertpress.com**.